LATINO ETHNIC CONSCIOUSNESS

LATINO ETHNIC CONSCIOUSNESS

The Case of Mexican Americans and Puerto Ricans in Chicago

Felix M. Padilla

UNIVERSITY OF NOTRE DAME PRESS
NOTRE DAME, INDIANA 46556

University of Notre Dame Press
Notre Dame, Indiana 46556

Manufactured in the United States of America

Library of Congress Cataloging in Publication Data

Padilla, Felix M.
Latino ethnic consciousness.

Bibliography: p.
Includes index.
1. Mexican Americans—Illinois—Chicago—Ethnic identity. 2. Puerto Ricans—Illinois—Chicago—Ethnic identity. 3. Chicago (Ill.)—Ethnic relations. I. Title.
F548.9.M5P32 1985 305.8'68077311 85-8576
ISBN 0-268-01274-1
ISBN 0-268-01275-X (pbk.)

Contents

Preface

This study provides an analysis of the process of Latino/Hispanic ethnic group formation in the city of Chicago. It examines and explains the conditions that have enabled Mexican Americans and Puerto Ricans to transcend the boundaries of their respective nationally and culturally based communities and adopt a new and different collective "Latino" or "Hispanic" identity during the early years of the 1970s. In short, the book represents an attempt at a systematic analysis of the interaction process involving Puerto Ricans and Mexican Americans in the city of Chicago which has led to the manifestation and expression of a Latino or Hispanic ethnic-conscious identity and behavior, distinct and separate from the groups' individual ethnic identities.

The decision to discuss the concept of Latino in ethnic terms was dictated by both personal and intellectual reasons. First, serving as one reason is my own practical experience in Chicago, where, as a second-generation Puerto Rican, I participated with other non-Puerto Rican, Spanish-speaking individuals in Latino-related activities. Participation in these various communal activities provided the context from which to observe the manifestation and expression of a collective Latino- or Hispanic-conscious identity and behavior. And, second, I was further influenced by a growing interest in developing an appropriate theoretical framework for the study of this collective group form comprised of a multi-ethnic population.

For those concerned with the systematic analysis of Latino or Hispanic ethnic identity and behavior, case studies of Chicago's Spanish-speaking groups offer several obvious heuristic advantages. The history of a collectivity of Spanish-speaking groups in Chicago is longer than the history of any numerically equalled aggregation of Spanish-speakers in most other American cities. In urban areas of the Northeast, Southwest, and Southeast one group has traditionally represented the leading or most numerous Spanish-speaking population of the area, i.e., Puerto Ricans, Mexican Americans, and Cubans, respectively. Further, most theoretical approaches used in the analysis of these individual groupings may be invalid when applied to the experience of Spanish-speaking people in the aggregate. And, finally, the history of this multiethnic, Spanish-speaking collectivity offers a wealth of empirical evidence. With this evidence it is possible to construct and test simple models for the study of "Latino or Hispanic identity."

I want to acknowledge several of the many individuals who helped me to clarify and refine my ideas. Among those who graciously gave of their knowledge and time are two outstanding teachers and scholars, James P. Pitts and Albert Hunter of Northwestern University. Dr. Samuel Betances, Northeastern Illinois University, who was a teacher and now a colleague and friend, spent long hours discussing with me the idea of a Latino or Hispanic identity and his views on the different Spanish-speaking groups' reaction to it.

Several other people deserve special thanks. Howard Becker, who chaired my dissertation committee and guided my work, was a constant source of ideas and inspiration. My stimulating discussions with Susan Olzak, University of Georgia, and Joane Nagel, University of Kansas, forced me to redefine my theoretical positions. Their brilliant, precise article "Ethnic Mobilization in New and Old States: An Extension of the Competitive Model" introduced me to works that had a profound influence on my writing. I want to thank Marilyn Perlberg, my assistant at the Center for

Latino and Latin American Affairs, Northern Illinois University, for her excellent job of editing and typing earlier drafts of the manuscript. Faith M. Kunkel, my right hand person at the center for the last year and the person most responsible for keeping "things in order" there, is also commended for putting up with the many other drafts of the manuscript and finally typing its final form.

Many thanks go to the editor of the *Social Science Quarterly Journal* for his permission to use material which appeared originally in that journal, although in somewhat different form.

And, finally, but not least, I wish to acknowledge the love and support of my wife, Beatrice. Her understanding of the work and of my constant absences from home for the last several years has made the completion of this project much easier.

Introduction

This book is a study of the concept of Hispanic or Latino as a form of (what shall be termed in this study) an ethnic-conscious identity and behavior, distinct and separate from the individual ethnic identity of Mexican Americans, Puerto Ricans, Cubans, and other Spanish-speaking groups. Its focus is Chicago's Mexican American and Puerto Rican populations. The attempt here is an investigation and analysis of certain external and internal factors and conditions which have led to the ethnic change manifest in the emergence of this "new" Latino or Hispanic ethnic identity in an American urban setting. In more specific terms, the study combines historical data (i.e., organization archives, accounts found in the literature, newspaper articles, and other relevant information) with interviews of community organization leaders to (1) provide a definition of the concept of Latino or Hispanic and (2) reconstruct the sequence of developments in American and Spanish-speaking institutions and organizations which helps to explain the process by which the concept of Hispanic or Latino has become another form of ethnic group identity and consciousness in the city of Chicago.[1]

This research was greatly influenced by the fact that the concept of Latino or Hispanic (to be also referred here as Latinismo or Hispanismo) is being drawn more and more to the attention of increasing numbers of people in the United States. As Spanish-speaking people identify themselves and others in the idiom of Latino similarity and/or differences, it is clear that this type of group identification means quite different things to different people—Latinismo may be simply considered a slippery term.

Further, there is little conceptual precision on the meaning of Latinismo when used as an expression of a wider identity for Spanish-speaking groups. In fact, it has become common for social scientists to refer to these populations, either as individual ethnics or as a collectivity, as "Latinos" without an explanation of the process by which they are "Latinocized." To this day social scientists have failed to make a conceptual distinction between behavior which is Latino- or Hispanic-related and that which is the expression of individual and separate Spanish-speaking ethnics.[2] In effect, social-science research has taken for granted the specific changes of ethnic identification among the various Spanish-speaking groups which at times result in the manifestation of a distinct and all-embracing Latino or Hispanic ethnic identity and consciousness.

By using the concept of Latino synonymously with the individual experiences of separate Spanish-speaking ethnics, social-science research has failed to examine the empirical characteristics and boundaries of Latino identity and solidarity and the important issues which an investigation of this type of group identification may raise. This focus, moreover, has detracted from an examination of the forces in the larger society that may encourage and spark the emergence of Latino ethnic identity and solidarity. And, finally, this one-dimensional perspective has neglected the shared political history of Mexican Americans and Puerto Ricans and other Spanish-speaking groups, thus obscuring such innovations as Latinismo or Hispanismo which may develop in these shared-political contexts.

In direct contrast I argue that it is too simple to assume that behavioral phenomena relating to individual and separate Mexican American, Puerto Rican, Cuban, and Central and South American groups are necessarily expressions of Latino consciousness. In the first place, the degree of correspondence, if any, should be tested empirically and not assumed a priori. In the second place, the difference between behavior that is an expression of Latino consciousness and that which is either Mexican American, Puerto Rican, Cuban, and the like ought to be reconciled by an appropriate theory.

The present study will attempt to fill this gap. First, it will show that Hispanismo or Latinismo represents a collective-generated ethnic group identity and behavior, that is, a type of identification and behavior which is produced out of the intergroup relations or social interaction of at least two Spanish-speaking groups. The Latino identity-formation process entails, at its most basic form, a process through which two or more Spanish-surnamed ethnics cross their individual group boundaries and seek solidarity as a wider Latino unit. When defined as emanating from the social interaction of two or more ethnic groups of Spanish-speakers, the Latino boundary becomes variable.* In other words, it will be argued that the apparently reducible principle of a "sense of Latino ethnic identity" must be presumed to vary correspondingly, and to be reducible, after all, to the structural factors which are commonly shared by some Spanish-speaking populations and which are subsequently responsible for affecting and regulating relations among them. By structural factors I mean those particular conditions which Spanish-speaking groups experience in common at the city-wide level. Discrimination in education and employment, for instance, represent some of the structural commonalities shared by Spanish-speaking ethnics. In contrast, there are other factors which are community-based (i.e., discrimination in housing), which do not provide the basis for intergroup relations among Spanish-surnamed populations. That is, community-based involvements or issues do not necessitate the expression of a wider Latino frame. Since

*The term "Latino boundary" is used here to mean the same as a wider scale unit or frame comprised of more than one Spanish-speaking population.

Mexican Americans and Puerto Ricans in Chicago live in geographic spatial communities (a descriptive analysis of these distinct populations and communities is presented in chapter 2), there are certain things that are restricted to the ethnic experience of a particular community, while there are others which are widely shared by residents of the various Spanish-surnamed areas. In effect, the structural dimension of Latino ethnic identification refers to the restraints enjoined upon the various Spanish-speaking groups as a consequence of the various systems of inequality of the larger American society. The important point to bear in mind is that the inequality experience shared by Spanish-speaking ethnics from different geographically located communities in areas such as education and employment provides the overall structural framework of social relations among some of these groups.

In reference to this view, it will be further shown that the manifestation and salience of Latino ethnic-conscious identity and solidarity are operative within specific situational contexts or at certain times in the urban life of Spanish-speaking groups. In short, the Latino or Hispanic ethnic boundary and cleavage represents a specific case of *situational ethnic identity*. This means that this multiethnic unit is fabricated and becomes most appropriate or salient for social action during those particular situations or moments when two or more Spanish-speaking ethnic groups are affected by the structural forces noted above and mobilize themselves as one to overcome this impact. (This point will be further elaborated below.) Conversely, there are other situational contexts when the "individual national" identification of a particular group (i.e., Mexican American, Puerto Rican, or Cuban) is more suitable for mobilization. In this way ethnic behavior among Spanish-speaking groupings can be expressed in an individual national form or as a wider Latino unit. Overall, the underlying assumption in situational Latino ethnic-conscious identity and behavior is that certain contexts and forces determine when members of distinctive and separate Spanish-speaking groups may pursue a course of action either as "Latinos" or as individual

Mexican Americans, Puerto Ricans, Cubans, and others. As in the expression of these distinct national identities, the manifestation of Latino solidarity leads to a specific degree of regularity in social behavior and action as one wider unit, and it is for this reason that we can make an analytic distinction between behavior which is Latino-related and that which is Mexican American-, Puerto Rican-, or Cuban-related. Further, regularities in the expression of Latino behavior are a direct indication of the process of intergroup relations between Mexican Americans, Puerto Ricans, Cubans, and other Spanish-speaking groupings.

Second, the book will present two different attempts made in the city of Chicago during the early 1970s to unite people with different ethnic identities (Mexican Americans and Puerto Ricans) under one Latino ethnic unit.[3] Each case involves the assertion that the Latino ethnic identity is more significant for certain purposes than individual cultural affiliations or national origin, while at the same time maintaining that the two ethnic identities are not lost or replaced by the "taking-on" of a wider Latino identity. In short, the two cases discuss efforts to create a new Latino or Hispanic ethnic identity that would serve to unite people previously holding quite distinctive identifications. Equally important, I shall use the two different cases not only to describe the process of Latino ethnic-identity formation in Chicago but also to develop an analytic framework that can provide explanation and analysis of the direction of ethnic change among Spanish-speaking people in other cities in the United States or even at the national level.

In sum, the study advances the concept of Latino as an "ethnic principle of organization." Such a notion is generated out of a myth of common origin (based on language similarity) and broader social conditions not in themselves "ethnic" at all. Latino ethnicity is fabricated out of shared cultural and structural similarities and functions according to the needs of Spanish-speaking groups. (A more elaborate discussion of Latino ethnicity is presented in chapter 5.)

The thesis of this analysis is comprised of two essential

points. First, it will be argued that the emergence and growth of Latino ethnic identity and consciousness in Chicago have been heavily influenced by the degree or level of integration of Spanish-speaking groups in the institutional life of American society. (The term "integration" is used here in the limited meaning of participation—full or marginal—in the important institutions of the larger society that need not be followed by assimilation in the usual sense of cultural merger.) I shall argue that the degree of integration of an ethnic group in the institutional life of the larger society determines, in part, the kinds of strategies or cultural innovations that such a group would create to relate to circumstances of societal inequality. The establishment of the concept of Latino as a wider identity is one such cultural creation.

In general this examination is based on the premise that, on the one hand, ethnic identities in this country have been shaped and/or accelerated by the transformation of America into an industrial society with its different phases of development. On the other hand, the advent of industrial growth and expansion created a "dual labor market" that allowed the full integration of some groups, while marginally or peripherally linking other groups to this and other major institutions of society. In other words, the dual labor market divided the work force into two groups: one employed in sheltered (primary) markets—characterized by systems of internal training and promotion, great job security, and high wages—the other crowded into "secondary" markets with low-wage, dead-end, short-term jobs (see Weiskoff, 1972; Bowles, 1973; Gordon, 1971; Reich, 1977; and Zellner, 1972). Viewed differently, the process of industrialization forged an economic order which created an unevenness in the distribution of ethnic groups in the division of labor: one or more ethnic groups occupy the prestige positions in a society, while other ethnics occupy the less desirable.

For the growing numbers of Puerto Rican and Mexican American city residents less desirable occupations have defined and afforded their participation in the institutional life of American society: for these groups integration has come to mean relegation to economically less productive and increasingly marginal positions in the urban labor force. This form of integration has subjected large portions of the Spanish-speaking populations to a distinct configuration of ethnic constraints and social change. They have been forced to adjust the ways they relate to work, family ties, and religion, and in some cases they have had to innovate by creating new institutions and cultural symbols that relate to the current circumstances of inequality. From this point of view Latino ethnic-conscious behavior is one of those important innovations that has been produced through and in reaction to the kind of integration that members of the various Spanish-speaking groups have experienced in American society. Thus, for the Spanish-speaking the creation of a Latino ethnic identity should be seen, not as the product of their past and present deprivations stemming from exclusion, but rather as due to their actual and on-going participation in occupations that have been concentrated in low-wage and less technically advanced and economically more vulnerable industries. The integration of Spanish-speaking groups in other of society's leading institutions parallels their participation in the economic system. I agree with Barrera (1979:196-97) that "the system of structural discrimination that forms the essence of [group relationships] exists first of all in the economic realm, but extends into political institutions, the education system, and all forms of social structure."

In effect, at the heart of Latino or Hispanic ethnic identity are the circumstantial conditions of structural or institutional inequality. Like the deprived lower classes of Marxist theory, some Mexican Americans and Puerto Ricans seek to redress their disadvantaged situation through a collective or large-scale Latino boundary. It is my view that institutional inequality, along with the pattern in which it is structured, is one of the leading independent variables in the formation process of Latino ethnic identity and behavior.

The second feature of the thesis advances the notion that the sharing of structural and cultural (language) commonalities among two or more Spanish-speaking ethnics is not sufficient to activate Latino ethnic mobilization. "Latino ethnic mobilization" and "identity" must be viewed as two empirically distinct processes: *Latino ethnic identity* symbolizes basic identification with a language population, while *Latino ethnic mobilization* represents the action or actual result of interaction among two or more Spanish-speaking groups. Latino ethnic mobilization (that is, the interaction process through which Puerto Ricans, Mexican Americans, Cubans, and others cut across individual boundaries and mobilize themselves as a Latino or Hispanic unit) has been excited or energized by certain governmental and public policies, resulting from the expansion and involvement of the polity in the social and economic life of American society.* In other words, the expansion of the role of the polity in American society and its creation of policies and "participatory programs"—as civil rights laws, equal employment opportunities, and affirmative action—facilitated the "connectedness," in Hannan's (1979) words, and scale of organization among Puerto Ricans, Mexican Americans, Cubans, and others leading to frequent interaction and mobilization as one "homogenous, language population."

Observers give different reasons for the expansion of the political center of today's modern societies. One view holds that the expansion of the political system grew out of the needs of industry and property capital. Levine (1960) notes that by the 1920s business interests had recognized the need for state intervention in the form of city planning and state funding of large construction projects to aid capitalist expansion. Citizen associations, dominated by business and professional elites "who were the owners and managers of the big department stores, banks, the office buildings, and

*The term "polity" simply refers here to the political system of the nation.

the trustees of colleges, hospitals, and museums" (Banfield and Wilson, 1963:268), lobbied for the establishment of planning commissions in a large number of American cities. With the outward movement of middle-class whites to suburban areas and the decline of production jobs in manufacturing after World War II, business elites in most larger American cities organized to prepare ambitious redevelopment plans to establish these urban economies as centers for service and finance (Banfield and Wilson, 1967:267). Implementation of these plans, they knew, would require municipal planning and federal planning. Heidernheimer et al. (1975:115) note, for instance, that this was a major motive for the federal urban renewal program which started in 1949.

The other perspective maintains that social issues such as poverty and racial inequality, pushed into the limelight by the civil rights movement and its repercussions, also influenced the involvement of the polity in the social and economic life of American society. Symptoms of social disorder in the growing ghettoes such as increased welfare demands, juvenile delinquency, and collapsing school systems became objects of public concern. During the 1960s a number of federal programs—such as the Juvenile Delinquency and Youth Offenses Act of 1961, the Economic Opportunity Act of 1964, Community Action, Model Cities, Affirmative Action—were initiated ostensibly to develop new ways of dealing with the urban problems of poverty, unemployment, poor housing, and lack of opportunity, or, in other words, to help poor people.

Employing an opposite interpretation, Piven and Cloward (1971 and 1975) argue that these programs were primarily intended, not to alleviate the problems of the poor, but rather the problems the poor were causing for government. They emphasize the role played by the urban programs tackling the threat of social disorder and forging a new power base for the national Democratic party. In other words, Piven and Cloward argue that local governments did not seem to be willing or able to absorb the growing minority groups into the political and economic structures of the cities, and their ability to cope with growing social problems was limited by their own fiscal concerns. Federal programs were thus seen as a way of reestablishing social controls by socializing the poor and by connecting them to the national Democratic party: "The Kennedy Administration began to cast about for other ways of strengthening its base in the cities. . . . A way had to be found to prod the local Democratic Party machinery to cultivate the allegiance of urban black voters by extending a greater share of municipal services to them, and to do this without alienating white voters" (Piven and Cloward, 1971:256).

In any event the expansion of the political system has redirected an "increasing proportion of societal activity (ethnic and other) toward the political center" (Nagel, 1928:9). Bell (1975:145) notes that as political entities assume a more active role in modern society, everyone knows where decisions are made and "whose ox will be gored." As for Spanish-speaking groups, certain policies and programs, resulting from the expansion of the political center, have enabled previously separate groups like Puerto Ricans and Mexican Americans to transcend their individual national and cultural identities and legitimate their claims as a wider Latino boundary.

This approach to the study of Latino ethnic mobilization is an outgrowth of the "development" explanation of ethnic change. In general this model premises that in countries like the United States certain processes and features of economic and political development promote ethnic mobilization. In terms of political development, which is basically the central feature of the theory most directly related to Latino ethnic mobilization, Enloe (1981) shows how the growth and effects of the American state (e.g., the civil bureaucracy, the judicial system, and the military and police) have in many cases shaped the identities of ethnic groups as well as influenced their mobilization. One of Enloe's illustrative cases is that of blacks, who in many instances have depended on federal and local bureaucratic agencies for economic and legal protection. "If the 1950's and 1960's was the era of extra-state politics for Blacks (through the press, cultural institutions, parties, legislatures—though of course also through the courts), then the 1970's represents a period of intense state-oriented politics for Blacks, thanks to notable expansion," writes Enloe (1981:131).

Similarly, Nagel and Olzak (1982) suggest that this "political construction of ethnicity" in both new and old states is intimately related to resource competition. Their argument, as well as that advanced by Barth (1969), Van deBerghe (1967), and Hannan (1979), emphasize how political and economic developments have restructured resource competition in ways that activate ethnic boundaries in most states. The common theme of the competition model is that ethnic mobilization is a consequence of the competition among groups for roles and resources. Specifically, Nagel and Olzak (1982:132) make the point that:

> Competition for jobs in ethnically diverse labor markets tends to become organized along ethnic lines. This can occur when employers try to lower wages or break up labor organizing efforts by opening formerly segregated job markets, thus producing ethnic competition for jobs. Or, organized ethnic groups themselves can attempt to corner job or commodity markets for purposes of economic advancement, thus, introducing ethnicity into economic competition.

The organization of a larger Latino ethnic unit is indeed a clear case of a mobilized ethnic contender. Latino ethnic mobilization represents an attempt on the part of Spanish-speaking groups to mount a competitive front in pursuit of emerging resources and rewards. In other words, there are certain situations wherein Mexican Americans, Puerto Ricans, Cubans, and other Spanish-speaking groups may find a competitive edge in Latino ethnic mobilization rather than as individual ethnics.

It is instructive to note that the emergence of Latino ethnic identity and action is related to the same process once assumed to cause the decline of ethnic diversity and significance in the modern state. The conventional academic wisdom used to claim that the spread of modern economic and political structures would defuse ethnic sentiments and ties. Hannan (1979:254) sums up this traditional perspective by noting that "ethnic distinctions within modern societies [were viewed as] vestiges of former geographical and social isolation. The process of modernization [was] assumed to subordinate such local loyalties to modern national and cultural identities." Similarly, Nagel (1982:2) notes:

> The processes of state- and nation-building had failed to manufacture national identities out of local linguistic, cultural, or religious affiliations. Indeed, just the opposite had occurred. Ethnic identity and organization clearly appeared to be strengthening in the face of economic and political development. This ethnic vitality was particularly disconcerting to social scientists because it contradicted what seemed clear evidence of integration.

In this sense contemporary society is a leading promoter and activator of ethnic assertiveness. Latino or Hispanic ethnicity adds a special case to this trend. In Chicago, as we will show below, the political center has influenced Puerto Ricans and Mexican Americans to politicize their demands as a Latino unit in a city-wide context.

In brief, the thesis of this study advances the notion that Latino ethnic identification is a mix of both internally generated dynamics and pressures from the external environment. Shared structural similarities and generalized beliefs about the causes (e.g., cultural or language discrimination) and possible means of reducing these circumstances (e.g., organization of a larger Latino unit) are important preconditions for the emergence of Latino ethnic mobilization. In other words, the claim that inequality commonalities are shared by two or more Spanish-speaking groups and the development of an ideology occur prior to Latino ethnic mobilization. This explanation holds that before Latino ethnic action is possible within a collectivity of various Spanish-speaking groups, a generalized belief (or ideological justification) is necessary concerning at least the causes of the discontent and, under certain conditions, the modes of redress. In the same way the explanation is based on the premise that Latino ethnic mobilization cannot be perceived as occurring without a certain external stimulus. The actions of some of the state's most visible institutions provide that necessary stimulus. State expansion, in other words, has provided otherwise ununited, culturally distinct, resource-poor groups with clear objects for efficiently focusing their collective hostility and frustration. When viewed as being historically and organically linked with state expansion and its resulting policies and auxiliary programs, Latino ethnic organization shared a striking similarity with Enloe's (1980:5) interpretation of political ethnicity: "ethnicity is political not just in the sense that it serves as a basis for interest group mobilization, but also in that it has been a critical ingredient in the creation, expansion and maintenance of the most potent political apparatus, the state."

The research of this study is divided into five major chapters. Following this introduction, chapter 1 provides an examination of how Puerto Ricans and Mexican Americans fared in Chicago's social structure as individual ethnics prior to the 1970s, when the first attempts were made to create a wider "Latino ethnic innovation." The discussion presented in this chapter is based on the premise that the understanding of the participation of these groups in the institutional life of the city as individual populations would enable us to become cognizant of the creation and development of a larger Latino ethnic identification.

In chapter 2 we will examine the various conceptual definitions of Latino ethnic consciousness and identity provided by the study's respondents. Major emphasis will be given, in other words, to the ideological formulations used in the expression of Latino ethnic identity and consciousness by Mexican American and Puerto Rican community organization leaders in Chicago. The integration of these ideological forms with certain structural conditions, which we will show in succeeding chapters as giving rise to this type of corporate group identity, will make it possible to grasp more fully the special significance of ethnic meanings and ideals that serve as the ideological bases of Latinismo.

Chapters 3 and 4 examine the Latino ethnic identity in the context of certain specific urban structural conditions which influenced its creation and expression in the early 1970's. Chapter 3 describes the process by which the idea of Latino became another form of group identity and behavior among Puerto Ricans and Mexican Americans, emphasizing the interplay between these groups' shared sociopolitical characteristics and the larger American social structure. More specifically, a particular case of "Latino ethnic mobilization" is presented in this chapter. Several of the leading internal and external developments in the early 1970's which created the conditions necessary for Latin ethnic mobilization in this Midwest metropolis are the focus of discussion. Affirmative Action, a public judicial policy designed to redress ethnic discrimination and inequities, was the leading development which influenced the emergence and growth of Latino solidarity and mobilization. This policy supported and, in a way, encouraged the organization of Puerto Ricans and Mexican Americans into one Latino ethnic population or community of interest.

The existence of a "legal forum," from which Puerto Ricans and Mexican Americans could make "collective claims and demands," resulted in the establishment of an actual Latino coalition. The Spanish Coalition for Jobs was an Alinsky-type of community organization comprised of Puerto Rican and Mexican American neighborhood organizations and social-service agencies.

Within the Spanish Coalition for Jobs were three crucial elements directly related to the emergence and growth of Latino ethnic identity and mobilization. The first two developed in forms of protest against Illinois Bell and Jewel Tea, two corporations which were receiving federal dollars to train and hire minorities in the public and private sectors. Refusal on the part of these two corporations to comply with Affirmative Action regulations led to subsequent Latino mobilization among Mexican Americans and Puerto Ricans to receive legally defined opportunities. The third element was the development of the "Latino Strategies for the 70's" conference. This event followed the Spanish Coalition for Jobs' "victories" against Illinois Bell and Jewel. The conference represented a particular organizational strategy on the part of the coalition to further the promotion of the idea of Latino unity and mobilization.

Last, one other condition instrumental in the emergence and growth of Latino ethnic identification and mobilization in Chicago during this period was the conscious role played by one political activist: Hector Franco. Hector Franco's role was crucial in convincing the different leaders that a "Latino coalition" made up of various Spanish-speaking organizations was more advantageous for advancing their collective interests than working as individual Puerto Rican or Mexican American groupings.

In chapter 4 we will examine the second most important organizational development among Puerto Ricans and Mexican Americans in the early 1970s to further spur the growth and salience of Latino identity and solidarity in Chicago. Major attention is given to the role of an external structure (an "American" settlement house) in influencing the development of a "middle-class" organization—the Latino Institute—and how the latter shaped the Latino group identity.

By way of conclusion, chapter 5 presents a theoretical model to further the study of the idea of Latino ethnic identity and consciousness. A set of new directions will be suggested for future research on Latino ethnicity as it develops in other parts of the United States as a national identity for Spanish-speaking groups.

1

Social Context of Chicago's Spanish-Speaking

The analysis of the emergence of Latino ethnic-conscious behavior among Puerto Ricans and Mexican Americans in Chicago begins with an examination of the general conditions that helped to shape the institutional and structural life of the city of Chicago prior to the mass arrival of Spanish-speaking groupings. Like many other American urban areas, Chicago was an ethnic city long before the arrival of Spanish-speaking groups. European groups such as Germans, Swedes, Norwegians, Irish, English, Welsh, Scottish, Italians, Poles, Jews, Greeks, and others, as well as black Americans, can be considered the city's early ethnic populations and communities. Chicago's population expansion began immediately after the Great Chicago Fire of 1871. By 1880 the city was the home of 503,185 residents, and within ten years this number rapidly increased to surpass the million mark, making Chicago the nation's second city. And, like most other large midwestern and northeastern cities, Chicago experienced its greatest growth during the great European immigration period of the nineteenth and early twentieth centuries. The 1910 Census, for example, showed that first- and second-generation newcomers accounted for 77 percent of Chicago's inhabitants. Over the years the city's foreign-born population, like that of the United States as a whole, reflected a steady shift in national origin. Newcomers from northern and western Europe predominated before 1890, especially those from Germany and Ireland. After that year southern and eastern Europeans, particularly Italians and Poles, came in increasing numbers.

The city's expansion during this period reflected not only a change in numbers but the coming of a mature industrial society. Before 1871 Chicago unquestionably outranked her rivals in western commerce (e.g., trade in grains and lumber, livestock and meat packing). Chicago's location as an important focal point on lake, canal, and railroad (e.g., east-to-west passage) offered additional economic activities. The capacity for growth shown by Chicago in these economic enterprises further stimulated the development of the iron and steel industries. By 1890 the city of Chicago was "the manufacturing point of the country, judged in gross value of products" (Pierce, 1957:64).

For the new arrivals from Europe as well as for those who migrated from other parts of the country, the developing city offered certain economic opportunities in commercial, industrial, and service occupations. That Chicago provided excellent job opportunities in the blue-collar, skilled, and unskilled industrial trades is explicitly stated by Nelli (1970:9):

> Whatever their place of origin, European immigrants and native Americans as well poured into the lake metropolis, lured by economic opportunities. The city offered work in packing plants, agricultural-implement works, stove factories, steel mills, electrical-generating plants, mail-order houses, railroad shops, clothing wholesale houses, building construction, breweries, distilleries, and retail stores.

In the process of industrial growth in the twentieth century labor in most major American cities was culturally standardized for white-collar work requiring a certain degree of educational training. In effect, the rise of white-collar jobs and the expansion of education represent two of the twentieth century's leading avenues providing a greater potential for fuller participation in the American society. The growth in white-collar work meant a growing number of clerks, teachers, medical specialists, engineers, and salaried managers in large public and private organizations. Trow (1966:438) comments on these changes:

> Since the Civil War, and especially in the past fifty years [since 1900], an economy based on thousands of small firms and businesses has been transformed into one based on large bureaucratized organizations characterized by centralized decision-making and administration carried out through coordinated managerial and clerical staffs.
>
> When small organizations grow large, papers replace verbal orders; papers replace rule-of-thumb calculations of price and profit; papers carry records of work flow and inventory that in a small operation can be seen at a glance on the shop floor and materials shed. And as organizations grew, people had to be trained to handle those papers—to prepare them, to assess and use them. The growth of the secondary-school system after 1870 was in large part a response to the pull of the economy for a mass of white-collar employees with more than an elementary-school education.

Correspondingly, the children and grandchildren of European immigrants began to attend public schools for the first time on a mass scale in the twentieth century, and they began to stay together in school for longer and longer periods. They initially learned skills suitable for clerical work—reading, writing, and arithmetic—and later in the century they learned the more advanced skills for carrying out the complex functions of engineers, professionals, and technical workers. It was the offspring of the more skilled blue-collar workers who often moved into white-collar work, but of course middle-class children had the best chance for finding such positions (Schneider, 1969:439).

Associated with the industrial growth of the city was the development of machine politics in Chicago. The city's political system represents another bureaucratic structure of the expanding industrial economy which provided occupational opportunities and facilitated institutional participation to cohorts of immigrants and their children in Chicago.

Politics in Chicago, as in most major cities in the United States, has always been based on service. Bargains, compromises, connections, patronage, and favors were and are essential ingredients of practical politics. This exchange model of politics, described so well by Gosnell in the 1930s, has served as the archetype of the political machine (1967, rev. ed.). In Chicago immigrants provided the most significant source of electoral support for the machine during and after its period of emergence. The expectations and demands of the ethnics fall into two major categories. The first are symbolic benefits characterized by demands for ethnic visibility in elective and appointive offices. The second category concerns what Downs (1973) has ominously referred to as the need for "cultural dominance," particularly over space (e.g., neighborhoods) and over cultural-transmitting institutions (e.g., schools).

As a whole, the expectations and demands that various ethnic groups make are usually achieved through the process of the "politicization of ethnicity." This means simply the use of ethnic patterns and prejudices as the primary basis for interest-group and political formations, building upon these to integrate a given ethnic community into the wider politics of the city and the nation (Kilson, 1967). To the extent that a given ethnic community was successful in so organizing itself, it could claim a share of city-based rewards, and through congressional and presidential politics, of federal government rewards.

Basic to the ethnics' success at having their community or neighborhood in Chicago included fully in the city-wide machine organization (the politicization of ethnicity) was the keen competition between the Democratic and Republican parties for city office, as well as the internal divisions between city and state factions within the Republican party (Gosnell, 1967, chs. 3 and 4). Unlike other cities where

Republicans or Democrats had a veritable built-in majority, no such situation prevailed in Chicago until about the 1930s. Both parties had to work hard for victory in Chicago, and when victory came, the margin was small. Ethnic communities were able to benefit from this competition between Republicans and Democrats, as they provided the margin of victory, and in return their communities were given political recognition and legitimation.

In general these are some of the major conditions that have shaped the institutional framework of the city of Chicago. We will examine, now, how Mexican Americans and Puerto Ricans as individual populations became integrated into this context.

MEXICAN AMERICANS

Mexican Americans are considered Chicago's first group of Spanish-speaking people, having arrived in the city during World War I. The large majority of the new arrivals established settlements in three areas of the city: South Chicago, Back of the Yards, and the Near West Side. According to Professor Año Nuevo de Kerr "the three neighborhoods persisted with one significant change. South Chicago and Back of the Yards remained intact, while under the pressure of urban renewal [during the 1960s] half of the Near West Side community had moved a few blocks south" (1975:22). This other area is called the Pilsen community. (Map 1 below shows the geographic distribution of these communities in the city of Chicago.)

During this period of initial immigration the Mexican population grew very quickly: in 1916 over 1,000 newcomers lived in Chicago; by 1930 this number increased to surpass the 20,000 mark (Taylor, 1932). By the end of the 1920s the greatest proportion of Mexicans was almost evenly distributed in the three leading areas of settlement where they lived interspersed among European ethnics, particularly

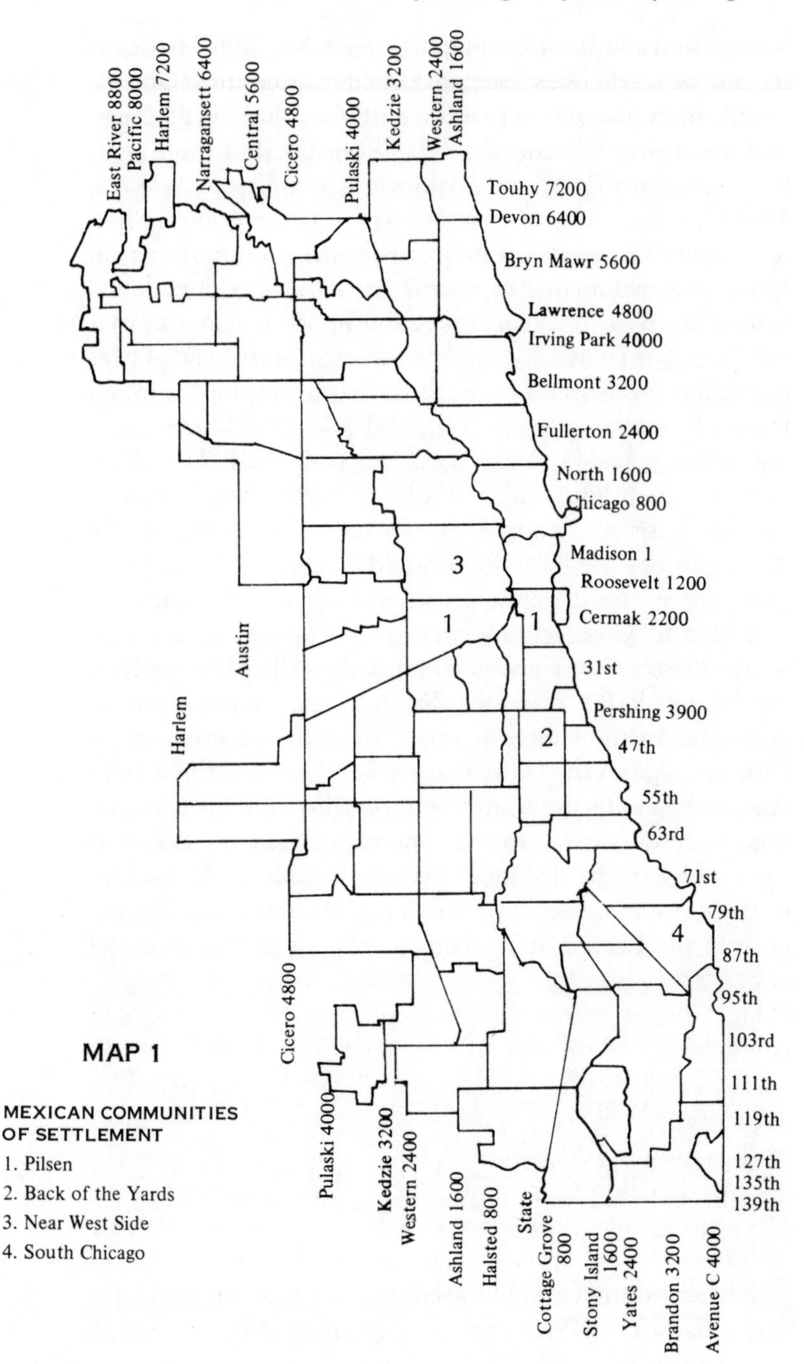

MAP 1

MEXICAN COMMUNITIES OF SETTLEMENT

1. Pilsen
2. Back of the Yards
3. Near West Side
4. South Chicago

eastern and southern Europeans. "Almost 7,000 Mexicans lived in the Near West Side with Italians, Russians, Greeks, and Poles as neighbors; 4,300 with Poles, Slovaks, and Germans in South Chicago; and 3,000 in Back of the Yards, primarily with Poles and Irishmen" (Año Nuevo de Kerr, 1976:28). As expected of newly arrived immigrants, Mexicans did not comprise a majority in these communities; in fact, it was seldom that they represented the majority population of a given block of a neighborhood or community.

The major areas of Mexican settlement were located near particular industries where the newcomers found employment: (1) South Chicago (steel), (2) Back of the Yards (packing houses), and (3) Near West Side (railroad). The Pilsen area, on the other hand, initially developed as a "seasonal stop-over for migrating Mexican families working in the Michigan beet fields" (Walton and Salces, 1977:17). Like many other ethnic immigrants before them, Mexicans immigrated to Chicago in search of job opportunities. The social and economic upheaval created by the Mexican Revolution of 1910 accelerated the large-scale immigration of Mexicans to the United States. This movement of people from Mexico to the United States had begun at the turn of the century with the completion of railroad lines connecting northern Mexico to the American Southwest. Primarily because of the distance between Mexico and Chicago, most Mexican newcomers had a certain amount of experience in the United States before arriving in this Midwest urban area:

> Unlike the immigrants who took the path to California or Arizona, the migrants to Chicago during the 1920's generally followed a northeastward drift from Mexico to Texas, then to farm work in the midwest, or to the packing-houses of Kansas City or to railroad track labor in various cities and finally to the industrial areas of Chicago. (Año Nuevo de Kerr, 1976: 20)

Notwithstanding this initial migratory experience, the large majority of Mexicans who comprised the first wave of immigrants to Chicago were overwhelmingly young, male, unskilled, and not prepared for the urban conditions of the new society. Many of the immigrants came to Chicago on their own, following the path described above by Professor Año Nuevo de Kerr. Most, however, were directly recruited by employers and shipped to Chicago via railroad cars. Once established here, those who did not work for the major industries of steel, railroad, or meat packing would often find factory and miscellaneous service jobs in nearby neighborhoods.

From the outset Mexican newcomers faced problems similar to those experienced by earlier ethnic immigrants: racial discrimination as reflected, for example, in residential restriction and segregation; cultural discrimination as evidenced by the treatment received by Spanish-speaking students in neighborhood schools; exclusion from participation in major institutions such as the Catholic Church; and the like. There are two other particular experiences, however, that make the Mexican immigrant case distinct from many others. One area concerns the job problem faced by the new arrivals and the other has to do with their citizenship or legal status.

The job situation of Mexican workers in the urban labor force was extremely difficult and complex. First, many of the newcomers, particularly those recruited by major American firms, were hired primarily as strike breakers and very seldom for permanent and steady employment. One particular case which clearly demonstrates this problem involved most of the Mexican workers hired by Swift and Company, located in Back of the Yards. When first recruited, these workers were promised permanent employment, but once brought here by the company, the newcomers were used strictly as strikebreakers. Subsequently, once management and the union representing the striking workers settled their disputes, the Mexican labor was immediately fired. The remarks of an employment representative for Swift and Company capture the fate of Mexican strikers during this incident:

> . . . the strike was broken. That was what we wanted to do and we give them credit for it. After the strike we let them [the Mexicans] out to let the old men back. No, we did not fire them [but we did not rehire them if they left]. (Quoted in Taylor, 1932:118)

For many of the Mexicans recruited to work in South Chicago's steel mills the experience was identical to that of Mexican newcomers to Back of the Yards. Although the steel mills provided the initial entry of Mexican workers into blue-collar occupations in the city, this initial entry was achieved through strikebreaking employment. The practices of one plant can be used to illustrate this point. During the nationwide steel and metal strike of 1919 various plants used an interpreter (a Mexican from one company) as an agent to secure Mexican laborers. The accounts of this interpreter provide insights on how Mexicans were recruited for the steel industry during this period:

> The companies sent me to get our Mexicans to work for them. I got some at Chicago, others at Omaha, Kansas City, a few at St. Louis. I even went down to El Paso and some cities in Texas. They were coming up here for over a year. We got some Mexicans for the Crucible Steel Company of Lorain, Ohio, and for Midland, Pennsylvania. There were other companies in Pennsylvania that got the Mexicans about that time. My steel company got about two or three thousand men that year. (Quoted in Taylor, 1932:117)

This form of participation in the urban labor force created a situation whereby Mexican workers were perceived and used by American employers as a weapon against striking and antagonistic laborers. And although on some occasions Mexican workers resisted this form of employment by joining ranks with the striking workers (Taylor, 1932), employment options for them were few in numbers, forcing many to accept those temporary jobs. This situation aggravated and accelerated the hostility of European ethnic workers against Mexicans, making recognition and acceptance that much more difficult to achieve.

When not used as strikebreakers, Mexican immigrants were very seldom hired for long-term tenure jobs. It became a common practice among American industries and companies to hire Mexicans on a temporary basis. This customary action was quite evident among railroad companies in Chicago. Taylor's description of Mexican railroad labor serves as confirmation of this employment method:

> Turnover is high, and there is a strong, ceaseless flow in and out from early spring to late fall. The jobs are often of short duration, and at their conclusion or before the laborers return to Chicago, soon to seek another job. The same laborer may be sent out to jobs by the same agencies half a dozen times or more during one season. Employment may alternate between steel mill or packing house and railroad. (1932:119)

Added to the dual problem of strikebreaking employment and temporary jobs was the problem of the low wages paid to Mexican immigrants. In other words, the job situation of Mexicans becomes even more dismal when one adds the fact that they received the lowest wages of all ethnic groups in the city. Año Nuevo de Kerr provides a detailed description of how the salaries earned by Mexicans compared to other workers' earnings in Chicago during the initial immigration years:

> The average annual income for steadily-employed unskilled and semi-skilled workers of all ethnic groups in Chicago in the mid-1920's ranged from $800 to $2,400, with $100 a month regarded as the 'poverty line.' Two-thirds of the Mexican households earned less than this $100 a month subsistence income, as compared with half of Black families and one-fifth of white families. This was despite the fact that a rather high proportion (47 percent) of Mexican women worked to supplement family income. (1976: 25-26)

In spite of these various strains many of the Mexican newcomers did manage to become part of the labor force of these major industries, though not on an equal basis with other workers and always as the last hired and first fired. The labor shortage influenced by World War I and the expansion of the city's industrial economy during this period created the conditions which led to a marginal participation or integration of Mexican laborers in these structures. For instance, Mexicans were employed as maintenance workers in significant numbers on the major railroad lines servicing Chicago. Taylor uses payroll records from 16 railroad lines to show the proportion of Mexicans employed in these companies between 1923 and 1928. His findings reveal that by the former year the percentage of Mexicans in these companies was 21.9; this number increased twofold (42.9%) five years later (1932:32). The corresponding numerical representations for these percentiles are 2,181 out of 9,978 workers and 3,964 of 9,238 respectively. The presence of Mexican workers was also felt in the steel and metal industry. Using combined data from 15 such plants, Taylor shows that in 1925 6,052 Mexicans were part of a labor force of 65,220, or 9.3 percent. By 1928 an additional 1,000 Mexican workers increased their numerical participation in this industry to equal 10.7 percent (1932:39). Although they were usually employed in the most unskilled jobs and paid the lowest wages among the workers of these industries, as noted above, the integration of Mexican newcomers in these structures has been viewed as analogous to the experience of earlier European immigrants. Año Nuevo de Kerr notes that it appeared Mexicans were following the traditional road toward assimilation in American life (1976).

Any hopes or thoughts of assimilation were shattered very quickly, however, by the major and most obvious and devastating incident of Mexican labor exploitation in Chicago, as well as in other parts of the country where Mexican immigrants had established communities of settlement. The incident was the result of the Great Depression, and it involved the collaboration of American immigration officials and welfare agencies from the state of Illinois and the city of Chicago in rounding up and returning Mexican workers and their families, regardless of legal citizenship status, to their homeland. This process, known as repatriation, was undertaken, according to these officials, as a relief measure. In other words, during this period the city of Chicago, as was the case with many other American urban areas, was perilously close to bankruptcy. And it became evident that money could be saved in relief expenditures by removing Mexicans from the welfare rolls. The sweep, however, included persons of long residence in this country as well as those of only a few weeks' tenure. United States-born children were known to have been expelled with their parents. Many American-born adults were stopped and asked for proof of citizenship, and some, reacting with anger as well as amazed incredulity, came into conflict with American officials. Belenchia's summary discussion of welfare repatriations in Chicago is indeed to the point:

> Some left voluntarily, as the general hardships of the depression were compounded by new welfare policies that limited aid to citizens. Others were forcibly deported, including families whose children had been born in the United States and were therefore eligible for relief and certainly would have been excluded from deportation in more prosperous times. (1982:123)

In the same light Año Nuevo de Kerr adds:

> After 1929 . . . repatriation was colored by growing antagonism toward immigration in general and toward continued Mexican immigration in particular. Aimed primarily at 'excluding probable public charges,' the U.S. laws made unemployed aliens especially vulnerable to the arbitrary use of repatriation as a means of lessening the 'burden' they were said to place on the public schools, jails, and hospitals as well as on welfare agencies. Mexicans had a higher unemployment rate than any other group in Chicago in the 1930's except Blacks; it was easier and less expensive to return them than it was to return Europeans or Asians. (1976:72)

Welfare repatriations became one of the most traumatic experiences of Mexicans and Mexican Americans in their contacts with American government authorities. No Mexican community remained untouched. The equivocal citizenship status of Mexican Americans and the consequences for their relations with governmental authority are nowhere more evident than in the actions of welfare agencies during the Great Depression of the 1930s.

In addition, the functional characteristics performed by the welfare repatriations of the 1930s provided Mexicans with some clear revelations concerning their legal status in the United States. First, repatriation emphasized the foreignness of the Mexican Americans. The intent to reject Mexican Americans as part of the normal American community welfare obligation was particularly evident during the Depression. And, second, the welfare repatriations of the 1930s were also a grim reminder that for low-status members of the group a claim to the rights of citizenship would always be subject to question.

Like many other ethnic groups, Mexicans responded to their conditions in Chicago by developing voluntary social organizations and associations. The dispersed geographic location of Mexican settlements in the city disposed these social organizations to develop primarily along neighborhood lines. Viewed in a different way, the early newcomers did not develop structures to deal with their collective problems. This point is very clearly stressed by Año Nuevo de Kerr (1975:23):

> The hardships of the 1930's did not lead to solidarity among Chicago's Mexicans. From time to time, it is true, there were such cooperative ventures among the settlements as the celebration of Mexican national holidays and the establishment of a speaker's bureau, but there were few attempts to discuss common problems or to represent those problems to the city at large.

In addition, most of the early Mexican social organizations and associations, like those of other immigrant groups, generally lasted a short time because of internal financial and political difficulties. Despite these shortcomings Taylor (1932) indicates that by 1928 23 Mexican organizations existed in this Midwest metropolis. The first voluntary associations were of the mutual-benefit type so common among immigrant groups. Many of these associations were established to perform a critical welfare role, that is, the associations worked to serve the Mexican community. Among these associations many performed purely social functions, and they still do.

One of the earliest and most notable organizations developed by Mexican immigrants in Chicago was the *Sociedad Benito Juarez*, or the Benito Juarez Club. Originally organized in 1918 by Mexican workers from the Rock Island Railroad Company near Back of the Yards, the *Sociedad Benito Juarez*'s major function was dispensing sick benefits to its members. As with many of the early organizations formed by Mexicans and other immigrant groups, the financial base of the *Sociedad Benito Juarez* was comprised exclusively of membership dues, usually a dollar a month. The organization also initiated a system of life insurance and helped in providing some of the urgent necessities to poor Mexican families who through lack of work or sickness found themselves in distressing circumstances (Año Nuevo de Kerr, 1976: 46-48).

Another earlier organizational effort among Mexicans in Chicago was the establishment of the first Spanish-speaking church in the city—Our Lady of Guadalupe in South Chicago. The exclusion of Mexicans from the neighborhood's Polish and Slovakian parishes influenced the decision of Chicago's Cardinal Mundelein to order three Spanish-speaking priests from the Spanish-based Claretian order to service Mexican Catholics in South Chicago. Initially the Spanish-speaking priests worked out of a chapel built by the Illinois Steel Company expressly for its Mexican workers. In 1928, three years after the arrival of the Spanish-speaking clerical order in the neighborhood, the chapel was replaced by Our Lady of Guadalupe Church. In addition to its religious function, "Our Lady of Guadalupe created its own social programs as alternatives for the neighborhood's Mexicans" (Año Nuevo de Kerr, 1976:102).

Another major organizational factor among Mexican

newcomers was the Mexican Consulate. The Mexican Consulate was primarily concerned with problems affecting the immigrant's legal status in the United States—it directed its efforts toward preserving the "Mexicanness" of its clients. And although individuals had little contact with the consulate, its presence was extremely important to the newcomers:

> . . . [its] most important task was to ensure the rights of Mexican citizens whose legal status in the United States was called into question. After passage of the Quota Acts of 1921 and 1924, Mexican immigrants were placed in the anomalous position of being among the few unskilled aliens still allowed to enter the United States. The tide of agitation against their continued entry rose steadily throughout the decade as a series of bills proposing the restriction of Mexican immigration was debated but not passed. (Año Nuevo de Kerr, 1976:59)

Along with these organizational endeavors, Mexican newcomers turned to settlement houses located in their communities for assistance and support in coping with the demands and obstacles encountered in the new society. Long-established settlement houses such as Hull House on the Near West Side, the University of Chicago Settlement House in Back of the Yards, and Byrd Memorial Center in South Chicago all provided facilities for Mexican community organizations, sports activities, dances, music, art, and English lessons. Mexicans usually did not meet together with other ethnic groups from the same neighborhood or even with fellow Mexicans from other neighborhoods. Año Nuevo de Kerr comments on the participation of Mexicans in the affairs of the different settlement houses:

> Mexican participation in these activities was limited and variable. But the settlement houses provided additional service. Mary McDowell, head resident of the University of Chicago Settlement House in Packingtown, was among the first to notice the entry of Mexicans into the Back of the Yards neighborhood. Within two years she began to include increasing sums in the settlement's budget for Mexican work, which in addition to instruction and meetings, included intervention in behalf of Mexicans with police and public health and welfare agencies.

> Meanwhile Hull House became a gathering place for Anglo Mexicannophiles. Well before the studies of Mexican villages which established his reputation as a major anthropologist, Robert Redfield did field work among Chicago's Chicanos and, along with other members of the city's academic and social service communities, attended events organized by or for Mexicans at Hull House. Thus the settlement houses helped bring Chicago's Mexicans to the attention of the larger community. (1976:53)

As the 1930s came to a close, the Mexicans who survived repatriation were few in numbers. Those who remained in this midwestern metropolis proved their intention to stay, whatever the obstacles. Further, the surviving Mexican families developed to be quite different from the way they and other families had been before repatriation. The most significant and dramatic change manifested in Chicago's Mexican population after the Depression was that it was "overwhelmingly young and American-born, . . . [showing] every sign of becoming Mexican American instead of Mexican in culture as well as in citizenship, and of following the traditional European immigrant pattern of settlement and assimilation" (Año Nuevo de Kerr, 1976:116).

Furthermore, on the eve of World War II the city's long-established and emerging Mexican American population was joined by a new generation of Mexican immigrants and migrants from Mexico and rural areas of the Southwest, respectively. The largest number of Mexican newcomers during this period were those who immigrated as part of the *braceros* (workers) program. Originally signed in 1942 as the International Bracero Contract Labor Agreements by the governments of Mexico and the United States, the *braceros* program was intended as part of the solution to the agricultural labor shortage in the Southwest created by the war. A year later the program was modified to include non-agricultural workers, that is, the program was changed to include recruits for industrial labor. This change made Chicago one of the major points of destination for Mexican immigrants.

Under the *braceros* program Mexicans were brought to Chicago to be employed as temporary laborers, the agreeable contract period usually lasting six months. After the life of the contract they were required to return to Mexico; many of the workers, however, attempted to remain in the city permanently, while others returned from Mexico illegally. During a period of two years (May 1, 1943–September 30, 1945) more than 15,000 Mexican *braceros* were brought to work in Chicago. The *braceros* program has been defined, in part, as a federal subsidy of agricultural and industrial labor (Maldonado, 1982:174), as well as a program offering many workers "an opportunity to familiarize themselves with an anticipation of return, legal or illegal" (Año Nuevo de Kerr, 1976: 123).

In any event, as a result of natural growth, the steady flow of undocumented workers paralleling the importation of *braceros*, as well as the arrival of Mexican American and Mexican migrants from other parts of the United States, the overall Mexican population of post-World War II Chicago grew to nearly equal the original number of newcomers found residing in the city before repatriation. Año Nuevo de Kerr estimates the number of Mexican residents in Chicago in 1950 at 24,000, the majority of which were newly arrived immigrants (1975:25).

During and after the war Mexicans and Mexican Americans in Chicago made very few economic gains. For some individuals in the labor force, particularly those employed in the steel mills and stockyards, employment became more permanent, and wages were higher relative to previous decades. Año Nuevo de Kerr, for instance, notes the disparities found between the city's Mexican population and other ethnic groups:

> Of the four groups of Chicanos living in the Chicago settlements in 1950—the first immigrants, their children, new immigrants, and Mexican Americans from elsewhere—the immigrants, old and new, fared better than the Mexican Americans, and for the first time compared favorably in average income and education

to the European foreign-born with whom they most frequently lived—the Poles and Italians. . . . Mexican Americans, on the other hand, . . . were receiving lower wages than either the foreign-born or second-generation Italians and Poles, despite the fact that they had more schooling than immigrants and almost as much as other native-born ethnics. (1976:136-37)

In general, Mexican workers as a whole lagged behind every ethnic group in the city. A 1953 *Chicago Sun-Times* story demonstrated that with all the efforts made over the previous decade, "in all of Chicago there [were] 7 Mexican nurses, 5 teachers, 1 lawyer, 1 dentist, [and] 1 policeman." The newspaper article also showed that school enrollment among Mexican children was shrinking even as the population expanded (in Año Nuevo de Kerr, 1976:155-56). Similarly, the 1960 Census reveals that in that year the greatest concentration of Mexican and Mexican American workers (20.8 percent) was found in the "laborer" category. Another 7.9 percent of the laborers were still employed as "private household workers," while another 6.1 percent were "farm laborers." On the other hand, only 1.3 percent of Mexican and Mexican American workers were found employed in professional occupations (see Table 1).

TABLE 1

Mexican Occupational Profile—1960

Occupation	Percent
Professional, technical, and kindred workers	1.3
Farmers and farm managers	1.2
Managers, officials, and proprietors	0.7
Clerical and kindred workers	1.6
Sales workers	0.6
Craftsmen, foremen, and kindred workers	3.5
Operatives and kindred workers	2.1
Private household workers	7.9
Service workers except private household	1.2
Farm laborers and foremen	6.1
Laborers except farm and mine	20.8
Not reporting (includes women and children)	52.4

Source: Annual Reports of the U.S. Immigration and Naturalization Service, 1960.

Through the 1940s and the ensuing decade many of the long-established Mexican individuals—the emerging Mexican American generation—continued to follow an earlier pattern of social relations and organization-building based on neighborhood lines. In other words, the city's Mexican population remained divided into geographic neighborhoods which mirrored class, generational, and occupational cleavages. Moreover, for Mexicans who remained in industrial employment during this time, trade- or labor-unionism became another major form of organizational response to their conditions in urban America. In South Chicago, for instance, Mexican workers along with Eastern European ethnics took part in the formation of the United Steel Workers Union. The packing-house unions in Back of the Yards included large numbers of Mexican workers. Año Nuevo de Kerr provides a concise description of the participation of Mexican workers in various unions throughout the city during this time:

> Long-time workers in Back of the Yards and South Chicago found themselves solicited as members of the newly-organizing industrial unions, especially after the passage of the Wagner Labor Relations Act of 1936. In December of 1936 John Riffe, Director and Office Manager of the Steel Workers Organizing Committee . . . told an interviewer, 'We have from 150 to 200 Mexican workers in the union. . . .' Organization of packing house workers took place more slowly than that of steel workers. Nonetheless, Mexicans were finally beginning to enter the ranks of organized labor—not as Mexicans but as American industrial workers. (1976:92)

Beside participation in worker's unions, in Back of the Yards the Mexicans became active members of Saul Alinsky's multiethnic neighborhood council. The Back of the Yards Neighborhood Council, as the organization was called, was formed in 1939 as Saul Alinsky's attempt to bolster the growing unionization movement in the stockyards by creating a sense of mutual dependence in the workers' neighborhoods.

Unlike the various organizational efforts noted above, several groups were finally established after the depression years to coalesce and politicize the different neighborhoods under one collective "Mexican ethnicity." The focus of these structures was Chicago's "Mexican American" population, and their major goal was the assimilation of this generation into the life of the larger American society. One of the earliest and most notable organizations of this kind was the Mexican Civic Committee. The Mexican Civic Committee was formed in 1943 by the Chicago Area Project, a local social-service organization which dealt with problems of juvenile delinquency in several of the city's neighborhoods. The major emphasis of the committee was developing Mexican American political leaders who could articulate and implement social and economic goals for the city's Mexican American population. In sum, most of the activities of the organization "were aimed at overcoming intra-ethnic and neighborhood differences among Mexican Americans in Chicago" (Año Nuevo de Kerr, 1976:149).

A similar organization founded by second-generation Mexicans in 1950 was the Mexican American Council. The council's major purpose was to integrate Mexican American residents of Chicago into the life of the wider society through education and organization programs and activities.

The major problem of these organizational efforts was inherently embedded in their programmatic goals and activities. By focusing on servicing the needs and protecting the interests of Chicago's Mexican American population, the organizations became isolated from the newly arrived immigrants and migrants from Mexico and the rural areas of the Southwest, respectively. In other words, although the new generation of immigrants came to play an important role as far as the future direction and assimilation of the wider Mexican community in Chicago, it was never made the target of the new "Mexican American organizations" of the period. In effect, the emerging Mexican American leadership of the 1940s and early 1950s failed to recognize that immigration brought with it conflicting needs, and indeed conflicting interests, which they could not represent or deal with as proponents of a Mexican American agenda.

One major incident is illustrative of this point. When the *bracero* program was renewed between 1951 and 1964 and illegal immigration reached its highest proportion in the late 1950s and 1960s, these new immigrants were not recruited to form part of the constituency of the newly established organizations of the period. Instead the newcomers were left to serve as further contributors to the divisions which already existed within the "Mexican ethnic community of the city." And after the *bracero* program turned into a permanent, often illegal and intolerable, form of immigration, and massive efforts to deport illegal Mexican "aliens" were started in 1954 under "Operation Wetback," there was no organized protest to challenge the inequitable treatment to which the city's Mexican community was being subjected. In other words, when actions to deport Mexicans to their homeland were taken by American officials in the 1950s and 1960s—actions that affected the entire Mexican community of the city—there was no organization or institution to aid those who wanted to stay in the United States, a situation resembling that created by the welfare repatriations of the 1930s. Any hopes and thoughts of assimilation on the part of Mexican Americans were cast in doubt after the actions of American officials during Operation Wetback, as "the Americans of Mexican descent who had been partially successful in entering our national life, . . . soon discovered that the favorable treatment of Chicanos in Chicago had been a temporary expedient" (Año Nuevo de Kerr, 1976:118).

It was not until the mid-1960s that organizational efforts were started to claim the allegiance of all of the city's Mexicans; a new era of general organizational activity began during this period. Members of the first generation of immigrants, second-generation Mexican Americans, as well as legal and illegal newcomers, all became part of the constituency of several community organizations. At a time almost coinciding with the official termination of the *bracero* program in 1964, several organizations were formed in Chicago with the aim of developing a Mexican ethnic community of interests. The geographic base or location of these groups was the Pilsen community; by 1960 Pilsen represented the first area of settlement where Mexicans and Mexican Americans outnumbered competing ethnic groups. Unlike South Chicago and Back of the Yards where Mexican Americans shared ties to their occupation—steel mills and stockyards, respectively—the Pilsen community was not bound to a single industry.

One of the earliest organizational efforts among Mexicans and Mexican Americans to create a unified ethnic solidarity group developed in connection with the Pilsen Neighbors Organization. Originally formed in 1953, in part by the Howell Settlement House, Pilsen Neighbors was built on the Alinsky model of pressure-group politics. During the formative years of the organization Mexican participation was few in numbers; however, by "the end of the 1960's many of the officers were Chicanos. They had developed a buying cooperative, housing and community development committees and a credit union" (Año Nuevo de Kerr, 1976: 195). In order to influence the creation of ethnic solidarity, Pilsen Neighbors formed coalitions of volunteer groups, such as youth clubs. This youth-club coalition, for instance, focused on a wide variety of issues such as health care, improved school facilities, bilingual and bicultural programs, job training, and social services.

Another community organization established by Mexicans to promote an ethnic solidarity among all of the city's different Mexican residents was *El Centro de la Causa*. From the beginning *El Centro de la Causa* housed a range of supplementary educational services—tutoring, college recruitment, and classes in English and Spanish. *El Centro* also helped sponsor other organizations such as BASTA (Brotherhood Against Slavery to Addiction) and the Chicano Mental Health Clinic. Año Nuevo de Kerr indicates that these and other programs were supported by divergent organizations ranging from the establishment-oriented Mexican American Council on Education (MACE) to the Organization of Latin American Students (OLAS) and the Brown Berets (1976: 196).

In sum, this represents a schematic outline of the various organizational undertakings adopted by the city's Mexican and Mexican American residents in response to their conditions in urban America. Of great significance is the realization by Mexican leaders of uniting under one ethnic community of interests the earlier-established divergent neighborhood groupings. This new ethnic innovation points to the common similarities shared by "all" Mexicans in the city, and it also indicates that the newly emerging Mexican leadership was more aware of the political importance of ethnicity and/or ethnic solidarity in American society. In other words, the new leaders realized that there was more to gain as one citywide Mexican ethnic group than as separate Mexican groups representing the interests of individual neighborhoods.

PUERTO RICANS*

Puerto Rican immigration to Chicago started in the late 1940s, increased substantially during the 1950s, and reached its highest level in the 1960s. Puerto Ricans immigrated to Chicago and other cities in the United States primarily because their economic situation had become intolerable on the island. American involvement in Puerto Rico, which had started officially in 1898 with the outbreak of the Spanish-Cuban War and the subsequent transfer of the island-nation from Spanish rule to American domination, transformed the institutional life of Puerto Rico to mirror that of the United States. Puerto Rico became a colony of the United States;

*The data used for this section of the chapter are part of a larger study presently being conducted by this author; see Padilla's *The Changing Nature of Puerto Rican Ethnic Consciousness in Chicago* (forthcoming).

Puerto Ricans were to become American citizens. Although all of the island's structures were radically changed, the economy was most severely affected. First, beginning immediately after the take-over in 1898, American investors through the collaboration and support of the United States government began to transform Puerto Rico's multicrop agricultural economy into one which relied almost exclusively on a single cash crop. By 1940 a different change was made as light industry was introduced to replace agriculture as the mainstay of Puerto Rico's economy. And in the 1960s petrochemicals and similar industries became the structural foundation of the island's economy. All these changes only contributed in fostering the creation of a large mass of unemployed Puerto Rican workers. In fact, by 1940 immigration to American cities and other parts of the Caribbean represented an "escape valve" which both American officials and the Puerto Rican government considered beneficial to the island's development and without which, given the patterns of economic growth that had been established through the introduction of industrialization, the rate of unemployment on the island would have been unmanageably high. Hernandez-Alvarez (1967) suggests that "had it not been for the withdrawal of one-third of Puerto Rico's population, the social force for change, which had been generated as a result of the revolution of rising expectations brought about by the [government's] developmental program, probably would have propelled the island's population into much more severe situations of unrest and conflict."

In any event, the large-scale movement of Puerto Ricans to Chicago after World War II forms part of the second great population surge to the mainland; the first surge occurred prior to this time, and it was directed to the Northeast, particularly to New York. According to a report by the U.S. Commission on Civil Rights the New York City metropolitan area was the home of 61,000 Puerto Ricans in 1940; by 1950 the number had increased by 400 percent to 245,280; and by 1960 it surpassed the half-million mark: 612,574

(1976:21-23). The allure of New York began to decrease toward the end of the 1940s but particularly so during the early 1950s. The change in this pattern of geographic distribution occurred as Puerto Rican immigrants began to seek employment opportunities in other cities in the Northeast as well as other places outside of the region, which included the Chicago-Gary area; Cleveland and Lorain, Ohio; Milwaukee; and other minor settlements (Hernandez-Alvarez, 1968:41).

As noted above, Puerto Ricans began immigrating to Chicago in significant numbers during the 1950s and 1960s. According to the 1960 Census, the first official enumeration of Puerto Ricans in Chicago, there were 32,371 Puerto Ricans living in the city. Ten years later this number more than doubled in 78,963 residents; the Puerto Rican population increase between 1950 and 1970 was, indeed, substantial. During this twenty-year period several sizable Puerto Rican *barrios* or *colonias* (neighborhoods), usually of a few square blocks each, sprang up in various parts of the city. Beginning with the initial group of Puerto Rican immigrants in the 1940s (see Padilla, 1947), Puerto Rican newcomers usually settled in or near the center of the city. In a series of articles for the *Chicago Sun-Times* Watson and Wheeler indicate that there were several major initial communities of Puerto Rican settlement in this area during the 1950s: Lakeview, Near North Side, Lincoln Park, and Uptown (1971). The two writers also add that another group of newcomers settled in the Woodlawn community in the city's southside. Map 2 below shows the geographic location of the leading communities of Puerto Rican settlement in Chicago in the 1950s.

In all of these areas of settlement Puerto Ricans lived interspersed among whites and in some cases among blacks; there were few all-Puerto Rican neighborhoods. In 1960 only limited sections of the original *barrios* held small concentrations of Puerto Rican immigrants and their children. For example, the census of that year shows that there was a total

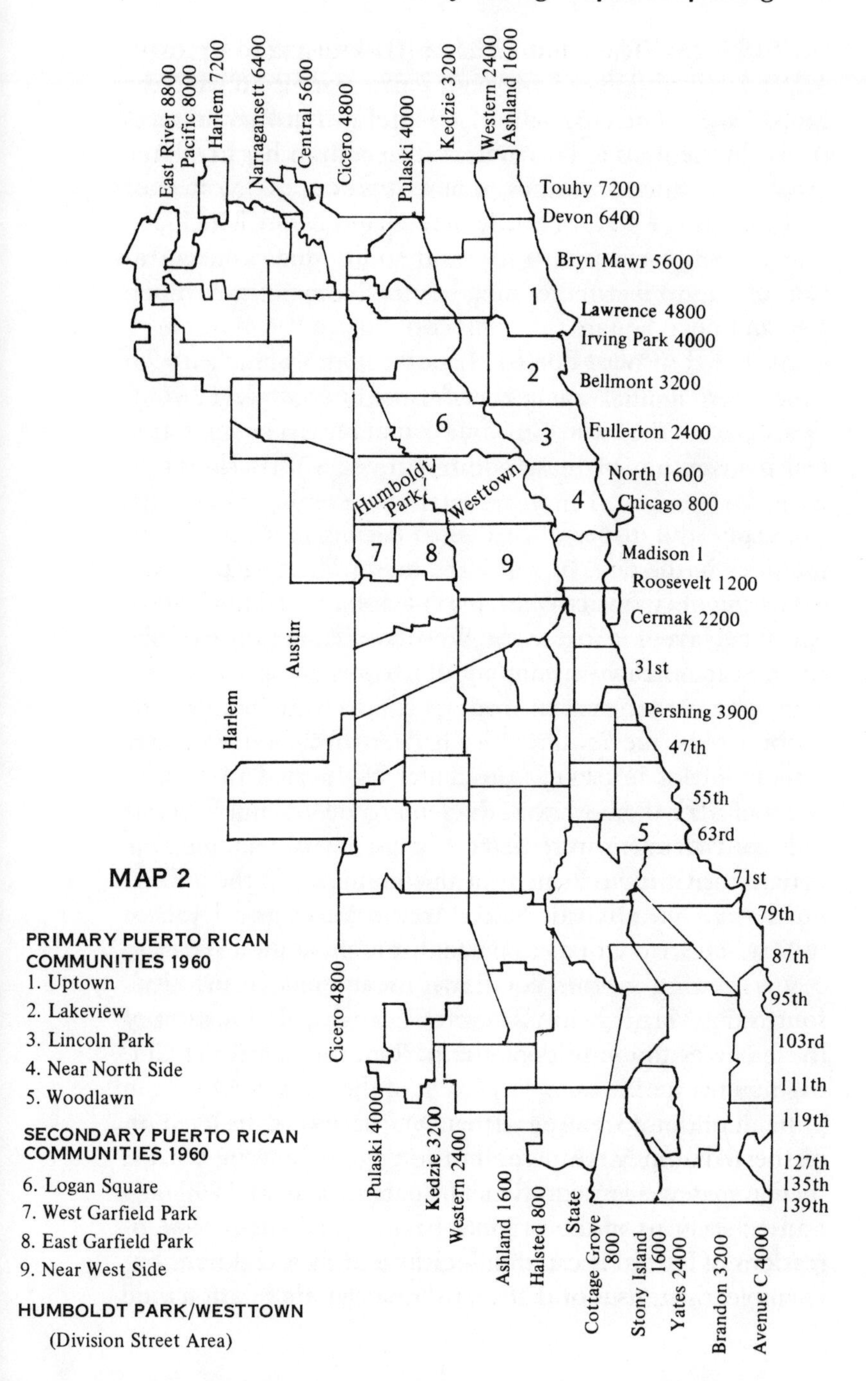
East River 8800
Pacific 8000
Harlem 7200
Narragansett 6400
Central 5600
Cicero 4800
Pulaski 4000
Kedzie 3200
Western 2400
Ashland 1600
Touhy 7200
Devon 6400
Bryn Mawr 5600
Lawrence 4800
Irving Park 4000
Bellmont 3200
Fullerton 2400
North 1600
Chicago 800
Madison 1
Roosevelt 1200
Cermak 2200
31st
Pershing 3900
47th
55th
63rd
71st
79th
87th
95th
103rd
111th
119th
127th
135th
139th
1
2
3
4
5
6
7
8
9
Humboldt Park
Westtown
Austin
Harlem
Cicero 4800
Pulaski 4000
Kedzie 3200
Western 2400
Ashland 1600
Halsted 800
State
Cottage Grove 800
Stony Island 1600
Yates 2400
Brandon 3200
Avenue C 4000
MAP 2
PRIMARY PUERTO RICAN COMMUNITIES 1960
1. Uptown
2. Lakeview
3. Lincoln Park
4. Near North Side
5. Woodlawn
SECONDARY PUERTO RICAN COMMUNITIES 1960
6. Logan Square
7. West Garfield Park
8. East Garfield Park
9. Near West Side
HUMBOLDT PARK/WESTTOWN
(Division Street Area)

of 581 Puerto Ricans and 122,595 whites living in Uptown; 1,191 and 115,018 in Lakeview; 2,699 and 50,569 in Near North Side; and 2,181 and 84,604 in Lincoln Park, respectively. In the Woodlawn community, on the other hand, the number of Puerto Rican residents totaled 2,055, that of whites equaled 8,450, while blacks numbered 72,397.

The 1960 Census also shows the fairly high concentration of Puerto Ricans residing in other communities in the city. In Logan Square the number of Puerto Rican residents totaled 561; in West Garfield Park the number reached 993; 3,676 lived in East Garfield Park; and another 7,162 comprised part of the Near West Side community. The geographical distribution of these additional enclaves is shown in Map 2.

Despite the dispersal of Puerto Ricans in several communities in the city, by 1960 the major Puerto Rican *barrio* or *colonia* in the city began to take shape. A large Puerto Rican enclave, located in the Westtown community on the city's near northwest side, popularly known as the "Division Street Area," was formed. (A smaller, but similar, offshoot in the Lakeview area also had begun to house another large number of Puerto Ricans during this period.) Although a few of the neighborhoods that emerged as distinguishable areas of Puerto Rican settlement in the 1950s remained the core of the Chicago Puerto Rican community in the following decade, the Division Street Area served new arrivals as the leading area of first settlement throughout the 1960s and 1970s. During the former decade, for example, nearly one-fourth (7,948) of the city's Puerto Rican population already lived in Westtown. In the latter period, on the other hand, this number increased to 42 percent of the city's Puerto Rican population, or 33,166 residents. Map 2 shows the location of the Division Street Area in the city.

The massive immigration of Puerto Ricans to Chicago and other metropolitan areas began during a period of modern industrial and technological growth and expansion. During this post-World War II "modern era" nationwide social and economic changes and technological developments were reducing the importance of manufacturing as a provider of new jobs in the major, older cities of the Midwest as well as in the Northeast. In other words, most Puerto Ricans immigrated to the United States during the historical period when the traditional unskilled and semiskilled jobs, which had represented the initial step or phase of integration into the American institutional life for large numbers of European immigrants, were in steady decline as major economic activities in many cities and were being replaced with white-collar and professional jobs.

For Puerto Ricans in Chicago this economic and technological growth and expansion has meant concentration in nonindustrial, poorly paid, menial, dead-end jobs. Padilla's (1947) study of the first group of Puerto Rican immigrants to Chicago in the late 1940s, for example, shows that many of the newcomers were employed in the restaurant business as busboys, sweepers, kitchen help, waiters, and the like. Others were employed in the business sector as messengers and delivery men; some in stockrooms and packaging areas of many stores. Yet another large number found jobs in the janitorial labor force of the city.

Further, according to one of the reports of the U.S. Immigration and Naturalization Service, by 1960 the majority of Puerto Rican workers were employed in three leading unskilled categories—"operatives and kindred" (45.7 percent), "laborers" (13.7 percent), and "service workers" (11.7 percent). On the other hand, only 1.6 percent of all Puerto Rican workers were part of the professional, white-collar occupations. Table 2 shows the overall concentration of Puerto Rican workers in the labor force during this period.

What was distinctive about these jobs, however, is that both white and black Americans tended to reject them in favor of more desirable employment. By 1950 most white Americans were fully integrated into the institutional life of the city, while blacks were beginning to improve their economic status in the trades and municipal employment. The two groups had little occupational contact with Puerto Ricans, who were concentrated on the lower rungs of the occupational ladder. Unlike Mexican newcomers, Puerto Ricans were not perceived as a major economic threat by white and black workers, and since Puerto Ricans constituted a rather small proportion of the city population, they tended to be relatively invisible to the larger society.

This period of fluid race/ethnic relations between Puerto Ricans and other groups in Chicago proved to be short-lived. As the physical Puerto Rican *barrio* expanded and the population increased rapidly during the late 1950s and 1960s, Puerto Ricans became evermore conspicuous, and the indifference with which they had been regarded in the early years changed to hostility. Ethnic tensions, police brutality, and the rise of a racist doctrine, which whites applied to Puerto Ricans, began to determine the status of the city's Puerto Rican population. The important point to note here is that since the employment of Puerto Ricans in noncompetitive economic sectors caused very little friction with white workers, racial/ethnic antagonisms between the two groups became related to social, political, and community-related concerns.

TABLE 2

Puerto Rican Occupational Profile—1960

Occupation	Percent
Professional, technical, and kindred workers	1.6
Farmers and farm managers	0.0
Managers, officials, and proprietors	1.2
Clerical and kindred workers	5.2
Sales workers	1.8
Craftsmen, foremen, and kindred workers	9.0
Operatives and kindred workers	45.7
Private household workers	0.0
Service workers except private household	11.7
Farm laborers and foremen	0.5
Laborers except farm and mine	13.7
Not reporting (includes women and children)	9.0

Source: Annual Reports of the U.S. Immigration and Naturalization Service, 1960.

From the outset, housing discrimination and police injustice became the leading forces responsible for fostering an antagonistic group relationship between Puerto Ricans and whites. As for the former, Puerto Ricans were trapped in the most deteriorated or run-down residential sections in their communities of settlement not only because of poverty but also because of a stringent pattern of housing discrimination. Suttles' discussion of a Puerto Rican enclave in the Near West Side is one example of the housing conditions experienced by some Puerto Ricans in Chicago (1968: 148-49):

> It is fairly easy to see why the Puerto Ricans . . . were able to first establish themselves on Harrison and Ashland. Along Harrison the buildings are probably the most deteriorated of any in the area and have long been blighted by the area's heaviest concentration of industry. The east side of Ashland is flanked by a line of old mansions that are inappropriate to the income level of local people. These mansions have been divided and subdivided into numerous flats. At the same time, both the mansions on Ashland and the apartment houses on Harrison are so huge that they are outside the range of local ownership. Thus, a lack of local ownership and a scarcity of other renters opened them to Puerto Ricans.

Further, the unwillingness of whites to tolerate Puerto Ricans as neighbors had similar, far-reaching results. And since Puerto Ricans were so limited in their choice of housing, they were forced to pay higher rents in those buildings that were open to them. Some landlords began to divide up large buildings into smaller "kitchenette units"—usually two or three rooms each. An owner of a building with large apartments could increase his income substantially by renting "kitchenettes" to ten or twelve families rather than to five or six families. A former resident of the Puerto Rican *barrio* of Woodlawn offers an account of the particular housing conditions faced by many Puerto Ricans in this area:

> I came to Chicago in 1952 and lived in *la barriada 63* [the neighborhood on 63rd street]. In those days, it was difficult

for Puerto Ricans to find large and decent apartments. I ended up renting a kitchenette apartment, a three-room apartment which was originally six rooms but it had been divided up for Puerto Rican families. When my family arrived from Puerto Rico, I rented another kitchenette in the same building because I could not find an apartment anywhere else. We lived like this for quite some time.

The nature of group relationship between Puerto Ricans and whites in Chicago was also heavily influenced by the actions of the police toward *barrio* residents. Initially policemen treated Puerto Ricans in Chicago with a great deal of resentment and enmity; Puerto Ricans became victims of racist and brutal police actions in the city. During the period of adjustment to the new society many of the newcomers were arrested for merely standing on corners or in front of their homes. Others were jailed for similar minor charges. For instance, there were cases when policemen arrested some of the immigrants because when questioned about their names and citizenship status, they would use two last names in their response, as *Mi nombre es Luis Rodriguez Martinez* (My name is Luis Rodriguez Martinez). The policemen would interpret this as another ploy on the part of the immigrant to evade apprehension from American authorities. Or the policemen would simply view this as a scheme to confuse them. According to many of my respondents not only were these incidents common in *el barrio*, but they led to many unnecessary arrests and embarrassing moments for Puerto Rican newcomers.

There were also different incidents of police brutality against Puerto Ricans in the city of Chicago, namely, cases involving the brutal beating of *barrio* residents. One of the most revealing of these cases involved the beating of two Puerto Rican men, Celestino A. Gonzalez, twenty-five years old, and Silvano Burgos, three years older, both of 2847 W. Division Street. The *Chicago Daily News* reported that the two men were standing on the corner of Mozart and Division about 11:15 P.M. on July 23, 1965, when the police came to chase children away from an open fire hydrant. Gonzalez and Burgos informed the newspaper that they went into their home as they saw the police drive up and were pursued by the officers who broke down the door ("Cops Brutal in Arrest: Latin Group," August 2, 1965). The two men were arrested and charged with aggravated battery, resisting arrest, reckless conduct, and disorderly conduct. And while in custody, they were callously attacked and beaten by the police. Gonzalez's account of the incident, printed in one local newspaper, provides further insight into this case.

> They handcuffed me in my room and took me to their car by pushing me and threatening my life. They took me to a hospital on Leavitt near Division where the policeman who broke the glass of my door was going to be treated. They pulled us out of the car and took us to a washroom in the hospital. There we were beaten savagely. The next stop was a park near the hospital where I was, once again, beaten up. Finally, I was taken to a police district where several policemen hit me like crazy; I fell to the floor and everyone that passed by hit me. I was bleeding terribly and I lost my conscious, when I woke up, I was in Cook County with my hands and feet tied to a bed. (*El Puertorriqueño,* August 11, 1965:13)

The Gonzalez and Burgos case created a flurry of community response among Puerto Ricans. One organization, which primarily helped Puerto Rican newcomers familiarize and establish themselves in the new society, complained to Mayor Richard J. Daley of the treatment Puerto Ricans were being subjected to by the city's police force. In a letter to the mayor the organization urged an investigation of this particular case. The letter also said:

> We by no means intend to give the impression that this is an isolated case. The complaints of Spanish-speaking residents within this area revolve around not only the several accusations of irresponsible beatings, but also a complete lack of concern on the part of the police in the protection of Latin-American residents. We would not mention this if cases could not be documented through witnesses from both the commun-

ity and various commissions responsible ultimately to you and to the city. (Reprinted in *El Puertorriqueño*, August 11, 1965:11)

This initial contact between Puerto Ricans and the white society during the 1950s and 1960s accelerated the growth of Puerto Rican consciousness in the city. The Puerto Rican ethnic identity underwent considerable evolution and growth, converting whatever residual regional town differences may have existed between the new arrivals into a sense of peoplehood. Manifestations of Puerto Rican peoplehood and consciousness were operative in a variety of ethnic-conscious attitudes and organizations: Puerto Ricans were forced to develop and staff a parallel set of personal and social services, neighborhood businesses, and communication networks to meet the tastes and needs of a growing Puerto Rican population.

The most significant response among Puerto Ricans during this period was their development of community organizations, several of which sought principally to provide guidance and leadership for neighborhood residents. The chief expression of social organization among Puerto Ricans during the 1950s and early 1960s was found, unlike the case of Mexican immigrants, in one particular organization, *Los Caballeros de San Juan* (The Knights of St. John). The significance of *Los Caballeros* among Puerto Ricans was first of all institutional, and only secondarily a matter of cultural transmission (as in the anthropological sense). In other words, *Los Caballeros* represented the primary means by which Puerto Ricans began to structure a self-conscious community for ethnic advancement and betterment.

The organization of *Los Caballeros* was chartered in the state of Illinois in 1954 as a fraternal and civic entity for Spanish-speaking men. According to its first executive director, Father Leo T. Mahon, the organization was designed to do for Puerto Ricans what other social agencies had done for European immigrants: "to help with work and wages, health and housing, with the difficulties of adjustment of an essentially rural population to the conditions of a city environment and to modern life." Father Mahon also realized that racial prejudice made the Puerto Ricans' situation in urban America distinct from that of European immigrants and engendered in Puerto Ricans a counterfeeling from a liability into an asset by directing the energies aroused by racial antagonism into constructive channels. In short, paralleling the aim of earlier Mexican organizations and associations, as well as those of European groups, *Los Caballeros* attempted to bring the Puerto Rican newcomers into the mainstream of the city's life while at the same time encouraging their cultural tradition.

From this point of view *Los Caballeros*' adaptive strategy combined some of the basic tenets of the assimilation and cultural pluralism theories often used by sociologists to discuss group adaptation and relations in American society. The assimilationist part of this strategy calls for a purposive attempt to become directly involved in the larger American society by adopting, to whatever extent possible, the customs, attitudes, and language of white America. The cultural pluralist version was based on the assumption that traditional Puerto Rican culture and socioeconomic prerogatives could be preserved in the face of white dominance.

To achieve these aims, Father Mahon outlined a concrete program of coordination, investigation, education, religious service, and labor relations that *Los Caballeros* attempted through the immigration and formative years. In order to attract and hold membership, the initial organization expanded into *concilios* (councils) servicing the different Puerto Rican *barrios* and *colonias* in the city. By 1960 the original organization, which was started in the Woodlawn community, had expanded into twelve *concilios*. These were located in the larger Puerto Rican *barrios* of the city. There were times when one particular *barrio* was the home for two *concilios*, as was the case in the Near North and Near West Side. Each *concilio* represented an ecological unit, a community of families and an organized church membership.

In general *Los Caballeros'* initial efforts were directed at organizing the different Puerto Rican enclaves into one politicized ethnic unit. The organization's initial program included provisions for recreational facilities and several social events, such as picnics, dances, baseball leagues, and the like. Since members overwhelmingly favored social activities, the *concilios* gradually placed a heavy emphasis on such events. The leading social event was the celebration of *El Dia de San Juan* (St. John's Day). Beginning in 1956 and lasting until 1965, all the *concilios* united to sponsor this event, which also included a banquet and dance. *El Dia de San Juan* soon became the major social event for the Puerto Rican community. Since its inception until 1966, when the event was changed to include the participation of newly emerging Puerto Rican organizations and institutions not connected to *Los Caballeros* and subsequently named *La Parada Puertorriqueña* (The Puerto Rican Parade), *El Dia de San Juan* was host for political dignitaries from the island as well as from Chicago. But overall this event signified the ethnic solidarity shared among the city's Puerto Rican population.

Los Caballeros increased the Puerto Rican awareness of their ethnic oppression; it heightened the expectations of Puerto Ricans about improving their lot; and it increased their impatience with existing racial/ethnic arrangements in Chicago. The oppressive conditions of many Puerto Ricans in the 1950s and early 1960s created the need for an ethnic political consciousness, but only an urban riot emerged as the initial antiracial activity of the period. The "Puerto Rican Riots of 1966," as the disturbances were called, constitute one of the most massive and sustained expressions of Puerto Rican dissatisfaction in the history of the city. They also represent one of the loudest expressions of Puerto Rican conscious behavior among *barrio* residents.

During the summer of 1966 the city of Chicago became the site of the first Puerto Rican riot in the history of the United States. These disorders began on June 12, 1966, when a white policeman shot and wounded a Puerto Rican young man, Arcelis Cruz, 21 years old, near the intersection of Division Street and Damen Avenue in the Westtown community. The scene at this intersection was intensified when the police brought dogs into the fray and a Puerto Rican was bitten. For three days and nights a Puerto Rican crowd demonstrated against police brutality. And each time the police tried to disperse the crowd, it only succeeded in arousing them.

From June 12 to June 14 Puerto Ricans not only defied the police but also looted and burned neighborhood stores, particularly those identified as white-owned. The city's Puerto Rican leaders pleaded with the rioters to return to their homes, but to little avail. In the meantime the police department ordered all available personnel into the Division Street area to quell the rioting, and on June 15 order was restored. By the time order was restored, 16 persons were injured, 49 were arrested, over 50 buildings damaged, and thousands of dollars of property destroyed.

The 1966 riots revealed that many Puerto Ricans were unhappy with the pace of progress; that the assimilationist strategy of *Los Caballeros* was only one form of integration into the institutional life of American society; that the Puerto Rican leadership of the 1950s and early 1960s, disciplined and patient, had its limits; and that the Puerto Rican rank and file, while Christian, was also human.

The Puerto Rican riots of 1966 were almost the natural outcome of the years of anger and frustration that had been building up in *el barrio*. In other words, the rise of Puerto Rican expectations became explosive and manifested in the disturbances of 1966 because of the dreadful conditions of ghetto life. (This was the case not only in the Division Street area but also in New York, Milwaukee, and other Puerto Rican communities of settlement.) Even more crucial, Puerto Ricans realized that these conditions could not be readily remedied. Nor could Puerto Ricans, by virtue of their minority status, easily escape from the ghetto, as did white immigrants before them. A state of permanent subordination and segregation— of social and residential immobility in a highly mobile society—began to loom as a distinct possibility from the mid-1960s onward. In short, the riots of 1966 on Division Street represented a particular attempt to call the attention of white society to the Puerto Ricans' widespread dissatisfaction with racial/ethnic subordination and oppression in urban America. Yet overall the riots heightened the Puerto Ricans' awareness of racial and ethnic inequality.

For the city's power structure the emergence of this racial violence and antagonisms and the increasing number of complex social problems operative in *el barrio* produced a need for social programs. The movement for social and economic reform for minorities, which had started almost exclusively for black Americans, was finally implanted in the Puerto Rican *colonia*. The federal government's "War on Poverty" programs such as Model Cities and Manpower Training became the official response to the Division Street riots. The first Urban Progress Center, established to serve Spanish-speaking residents of the city, was opened during the summer of 1966 a few blocks from where the riots had taken place.

These political changes grounded in anti-poverty programs were designed to resolve racial conflicts, but these changes did not significantly alleviate racial tensions in the Division Street area. In fact, there was a growing realization among many people that social services for the poor *barrio* residents were inadequate. Many services were fragmented, dealing with "parts of families" or "segments of individuals" rather than with people and their environment. Services were too often humiliating and degrading. Many citizens avoided the service agencies; others became "apathetic" or "bad clients" in reaction to the insensitivity of many professional helpers.

For Puerto Ricans the riot of 1966 helped to shift the philosophy of their struggle. In the postriot period the dominant pattern of Puerto Rican adaptation to Chicago's larger society began to give way to, or at least to coexist with, a more militant pattern of Puerto Rican political adaptation of interest-group articulation. *Barrio* leaders began to focus on more militant ways to erase the cycle of poverty, unemployment, and poor education. In 1967, for instance, the Young Lords, formerly a street gang, became the most militant organization of Puerto Rican youth in the United States. Most of the Young Lords' militant and notable activities occurred during the spring and summer of 1969. In May the Young Lords occupied the administration building of the McCormick Theological Seminary to publicize demands that McCormick and the city do more for the poor on the Near North Side where the Young Lords lived. A month later the Young Lords took over the Armitage Avenue United Methodist Church at 834 W. Armitage Avenue. By August they had opened a day-care center in the church basement. In the same month the Young Lords took over urban renewal land at Armitage Avenue and Halsted Street to make a "People's Park." The Young Lords also used physical force to break up a meeting of the Lincoln Park Community Conservation Council to protest possible use of urban renewal land for a tennis club.

At the same time community action programs of the government's War on Poverty, initiated in the Division Street area in response to the Puerto Rican riots in 1966, became the leading mechanisms for the institutionalization of *barrio*-based politics. Many of these programs were often transformed from community service agencies into local political structures staffed and directed by militant Puerto Ricans. These programs, many of which placed great emphasis on citizen participation through such bodies as "citizens advisory boards," were used to politicize the heretofore politically inactive *barrio* residents (i.e., welfare mothers, gangs, the unemployed, and school dropouts). The participation of *barrio* residents in community action programs helped to develop the political skills of a great many people who went on to manipulate political resources to influence governmental as well as private institutions and organizations. The leadership of Allies for a Better Community (A.B.C.), and Spanish Action Committee of Chicago (SACC), two of the leading militant groups formed during this period, had its start in the Model Cities service programs. These organizations, in particular, manipulated political resources to pioneer militant actions like boycotts and picketing for jobs.

The foregoing discussion points to the various ethnic symbols and innovations operative in the efforts of Puerto Ricans in their reaction to inequality in American society. In addition to the "traditional approach" of community organizing, by 1966 Puerto Ricans had incorporated a militant-type of group-interests articulation in Chicago. The militant ethnic consciousness shared by Puerto Ricans as well as the creation of an inclusive Mexican ethnicity by Mexicans and Mexican Americans represent particular forms of cultural innovations in response to these groups' unequal participation in the institutional life of the American society. In spite of these individual efforts the situation of the city's Spanish-speaking increasingly worsened by 1970. We will examine the collective experience of these two groups during the early years of the 1970 decade.

MEXICAN AMERICANS AND PUERTO RICANS AS ONE SPANISH-SPEAKING GROUP

Beginning in the late 1940s and early 1950s when the multiethnic Spanish-speaking population began to enter the city in large numbers, they confronted a society with established physical, political, social, ideological, and economic structures (the last of which, initially at least, was the most important). By this time Chicago's economic structure was old and rigid, lacking in the fluidity and openness which had characterized it about the time of the mass arrival of Europeans. Chicago's economic base had changed; technological occupations began to represent the mainstay of the labor market; and many of the traditional unskilled or semi-skilled jobs had disappeared, transferred after World War II to suburban areas or to cheaper labor forces overseas. In short, the large-scale immigration of Spanish-speaking groups coincided with a steady decline in the need for unskilled workers. For Mexican Americans and Puerto Ricans this kind of economy meant great insecurity and marginality.

In addition, the Spanish-speaking came to share with a large and growing black population the status of a "non-white minority," that is, they also shared the experience of being objects of prejudice and discrimination. Discrimination based on color immobilizes and effectively reduces the economic value of, say, education, to those discriminated against. Thus, individuals with identical educational attainment can earn significantly different incomes. Lower rates of return on education might well discourage investment in education by individuals in the groups concerned, who then might indeed suffer from an educational deficiency. In other words, it is unlikely that education can improve the situation of groups such as Mexican Americans and Puerto Ricans as long as discrimination remains to depress the return on formal training or schooling.

When we expand this relationship, we find that forms of social and economic discrimination—hiring and promotion practices in employment, resource allocation in city schools, the structure of transportation systems, residential segregation and housing quality, availability of decent health care, behavior of policemen and judges, foremen's prejudices, images of nonwhite minorities in the media and in the schools, price-gouging in ghetto stores—all interact strongly to determine the occupational status and annual income and welfare of nonwhite minorities. While the European immigrants and their descendants were able to move up the economic ladder and establish successful "turfs" in business, politics, the trades, and the like, and could take better advantage of the growth of white-collar occupations and the expansion of the educational and political systems, racial discrimination has stagnated the movement of Puerto Ricans and Mexican Americans from the unskilled sector of the urban labor force.

The situation of Mexican Americans and Puerto Ricans became that much more striking and apparent by 1970 when, along with Cubans and other Spanish-speaking groupings, they combined to represent the city's second largest minority group. The employment and housing conditions of this massive "minority group" were becoming seemingly visible. The official population count of the Spanish-speaking in 1970 was estimated at 247,857, with 43 percent or 83,000 Mexican Americans; 32 percent or 79,000 Puerto Ricans; 7 percent or 15,000 Cubans; and the remaining was comprised of other Spanish-speaking groups. It is important to note that several studies dealing with the Spanish-speaking experience in Chicago have disputed the figures noted above on the basis of undercounting practices by the Census Bureau. The following is an attempt at correcting the official count of the city's Spanish-speaking population of 1970:

> Beginning with the official 1970 Census figures of 247,857 and 324,215 for the city and the metropolitan area, . . . respectively, if we assume that the undercounted population was about twice that of the Blacks but, conservatively, lower than some national surveys, and use a figure of 16%, the corrected numbers are 287,514 for the city and 376,089 for the metropolitan area. (Walton and Salces, 1977:4)

In any event, the Spanish-speaking had become a sizable segment of the city's total population by 1970. But despite the growing size of the population, their integration in the institutional life of the city had not changed from previous decades. For example, according to the 1970 Census, in comparison with the city's total population the Spanish-speaking were grossly underrepresented in professional technical occupations. Nearly 6 percent of employed Spanish-speaking workers were in professional technical occupations, as against more than 12 percent for the city's total population. In the white-collar occupations the Spanish-speaking were also greatly underrepresented. In the category of "owners, managers, and administrators" Spanish-speaking representation equaled only 1.8 percent in comparison to 5.9 percent for the city's total population. This represents a ratio of one to five. The same is true for the category of "sales workers": 3.0 percent of the Spanish-speaking workers were found employed in that category, while the figure for the city's total population was almost twice as high at 5.9 percent. In fact, the census figures reveal that the large proportion of Spanish-speaking workers were concentrated in low-skilled jobs, with the overwhelming majority (39.8 percent) employed as "operatives," in comparison to only 17.0 percent for the city's total population.

The participation of the Spanish-speaking in government-related jobs was also marginal. This picture is clearly shown by Walton and Salces (1977:6):

> . . . among the hundreds of elected representatives to various levels of government in the metropolitan area there are only four persons of Spanish heritage and these occupy relatively minor posts . . . . Latinos comprised 1.7% of city workers and even less in important service agencies such as community development (.194%), fire (.15%), housing (1.9%), and police (1.5%).

Politically speaking, the Spanish-speaking have not been very important to date as factors in city politics since most Spanish-speaking live in wards where the machine controls the vote very well (Belenchia, 1982). In other words, Mexican American and Puerto Rican city residents are either outside or only partially linked to the politicization of ethnicity through the political machine. These groups have been deprived of participatory incentives, an experience that had motivated white ethnic lower strata's political development. This, in turn, has produced a Spanish-speaking urban lower strata that in the 1970s ranked low in all salient indices of modern political life: low political skill and knowledge, a high sense of powerlessness and estrangement from institutionalized processes, and low participation (see Walton and Salces, 1977).

Second, the city political machine's relative neglect of Puerto Ricans and Mexican Americans has deprived the elites of these groups (middle and upper classes) of the opportunity and incentives to give political leadership. Whereas the city machine's full-fledged inclusion of white ethnic communities provided a powerful stimulus to these groups, the Spanish-speaking elite has not been induced to use its institutions to politicize the Spanish-speaking lower strata in order to bring their votes to the service of the party machine. This is not surprising in light of Kemp and Lineberry's suggestion that "the dominating concern of the Chicago machine has been to maintain its white and largely ethnic power base, while accommodating the city's growing black middle class, which has numerous intertwined and often symbolic demands" (1982:7). Accordingly, it is safe to say that for both blacks and Spanish-speaking participation in the city's political machine has been controlled and limited until now.

In sum, the stratification of the labor force or the dual labor market imposed by the process of industrialization and racial discrimination in hiring practices, housing, education, politics, and the like have served to stagnate the economic growth and institutional participation of the Spanish-speaking in Chicago. In other words, these particular features of the American society became actual barriers for the Spanish-speaking, impeding their full participation in the institutional life of the American society.

Further, as the 1970s developed, the hardening dimensions of urban-based inequality (continued shrinking of the industrial job base) encouraged the creation of different cultural activities and symbols to overcome these conditions. Puerto Ricans and Mexican Americans responded to these conditions by organizing around a new cultural innovation known as Latinismo or Hispanismo. This cultural innovation was based on the premise that more could be gained or secured as one "Latino collectivity" than as individual Spanish-speaking ethnics.

This study will examine two of the leading "Latino organizations" developed by Puerto Ricans and Mexican Americans in Chicago during the early years of the 1970 decade. In chapter three we will examine the various factors that influenced the development of the first organization of this type—the Spanish Coalition for Jobs. And in chapter 4 we will analyze the process that led to the creation of the second major Latino innovation of the period—the Latino Institute.

2

On the Nature of Latino Ethnic Consciousness*

SITUATIONAL LATINO ETHNIC CONSCIOUSNESS

At the outset of this kind of discussion one is immediately confronted with the task of answering the following question: When is Latinismo or Hispanismo an operative group identity and consciousness? In other words, an analysis of the meaning of the concept Latino or Hispanic challenges the social scientist to examine when this group form is the actual expression of a collective ethnic identity and solidarity rather than the distinct and separate identities of Mexican Americans or Puerto Ricans. As a starting point I will suggest, following Professor Jim Pitts' articulation of "black consciousness," that Latinismo be viewed as a social product. This would mean in his words, "purposive action and interpretation of actions operating in social relationships" (1974:672). From this point of view Latino ethnic identification and consciousness may not be viewed as the product of individual Mexican American, Puerto Rican, or

*Part of this chapter appeared as an article, "On the Nature of Latino Ethnicity." 1984. *Social Science Quarterly Journal*, vol. 65, no. 2 (June): 651-664. It is reprinted here with permission of the *Social Science Quarterly Journal*.

Cuban groups, nor as existing independently of their intergroup social relations and behavior. Latino ethnic-conscious behavior, rather, represents a collective-generated behavior which transcends the boundaries of the individual national and cultural identities of the different Spanish-speaking populations and emerges as a distinct and separate group identification and consciousness.

In effect, the manifestation of a Latino ethnic identity and consciousness is operative when two or more Spanish-speaking groups, in this instance Puerto Ricans and Mexican Americans, interact as one during certain situational contexts. Conversely, this means that instead of representing the more common historically fixed or inherited type of group form and identity, as in the anthropological sense, Latino or Hispanic group identification and solidarity have emerged over time as a part of the process of intergroup relations and communication between two or more Spanish-speaking groups. Further, the expression of Latino ethnic-conscious behavior is *situationally* specific, crystallized under certain circumstances of inequality experience shared by more than one Spanish-speaking group at a point in time. Undoubtedly this type of group cleavage is also based on the effectiveness of the two groups' subsequent mobilization as one unit to seek resolution to their collective problem or to advance their interests colletively. (This point will be elaborated further in the last chapter of the book.)

On the whole, Latino ethnic behavior represents another form of group consciousness among the Spanish-speaking population in the United States. It represents the tendency toward sentimental and ideological identification with a language group. Latinismo also signifies the expression, in certain circumstances, of devotion and loyalty to the collective concerns of the Spanish-speaking, while in most other instances individual Puerto Rican and Mexican American ethnic ties and sentiments continue to shape separate group affiliations and loyalties. Viewed somewhat differently, the Latino-conscious person sees himself as a Latino sometimes and as Puerto Rican, Mexican American, Cuban, and the like at other times.

Members of the various Spanish-speaking community organizations in Chicago gave frequent and eloquent expressions to this type of sentiment. The following is a typical expression of this feeling of a situational-collective solidarity by one of the study's respondents:

> Here [in Chicago] we have a combination of different Latino populations; however, in each community the majority takes care of its own first. . . . I try to use [Latino] as much as I can. When I talk to people in my community, I use Mexican, but I use Latino when the situation calls for issues that have city-wide implications.

The remarks of another respondent, who discussed the building of a new school in one of the city's Mexican American communities, also reflect the situational dimension of the Latino-conscious person:

> . . . in Pilsen you have a Latino movement when they are talking or confronting the city. But in issues such as the Benito Juarez High School, you did not find a Puerto Rican being the spokesperson for the group that was putting pressure on the city to build the new school.

Another conceptual formulation of Latinismo as a situational type of group consciousness and identity was expressed by a community organizer from one of the leading areas of Mexican settlement in the city. A strong supporter of Saul Alinsky's organizing principles, this respondent sees this form of group identity operative in those instances when the concerns and interests of both Mexican Americans and Puerto Ricans are at stake:

> When we move out of South Chicago and South Chicago is to have a relationship with the Westtown Concerned Citizens Coalition, it will have to be around issues that affect them equally. We cannot get South Chicago to get mad at Westtown if Westtown doesn't support their immigration situation [the

issue of undocumented workers]. That is a Mexican problem that cannot be resolved through a Latino effort. But we can get them to come and talk to Westtown about jobs, about things that are hitting everybody.

In an interview with a newspaper reporter one of the first Spanish-speaking members of Chicago's Board of Education gives further credence to the emergence of a distinct, situational Latino identity in this Midwest metropolis. While speaking on behalf of bilingual education in the Chicago schools, this board member indicated supporting a "bicultural program which would provide the Latino child with a solid Latino identity, varying by nationality of neighborhood" (Chicago Reporter, 1975:6).

These various ideological expressions, as well as the ones that follow, suggest that there are at least two interdependent levels of ethnic organization which are in operation among Spanish-speaking groups: that which is localized in certain communities of the city (spatially limited) and that which encompasses the city at large (spatially inclusive). This is similar to Warren's (1956) distinction between the horizontal and vertical axis of community life. The horizontal axis emphasizes locality, and the vertical axis emphasizes specialized interests. Both spatially limited and spatially inclusive conceptual elements of ethnic identities are necessary ingredients for a complete understanding of the play of forces in the municipal polity which influence the expression of Latino ethnic identity and behavior among Spanish-speaking groups.

These various examples also point to the shift from a traditional cultural and national population-group frame of reference between Puerto Ricans and Mexican Americans to a behavior-strategy frame, which views Latino ethnic consciousness generating out of intergroup social participation. The perception of Latino ethnic identity becomes an understanding which has meaning for the social action of the people concerned, but this meaning clearly is contained in the social situation in which the interaction is taking place. It seems from these examples that the decision of Spanish-speaking groups about when to construct an inclusive or collective group identity and come to share a consciousness-of-kind as "Latinos" is based on the groups' assessment of their goals and their options to attain those goals.

LATINISMO: POLITICAL CONSCIOUSNESS

Politics is, according to W. Lloyd Warner (1941:301), the process through which services and benefits are allocated among competing sectors of society. Politics as such is to a certain degree central to the dynamics of Latino ethnic consciousness. Latino ethnic-conscious behavior is addressed to gaining access to American urban systems. The Latino ethnic identification, in other words, has much in common with what some scholars call political ethnicity, that is, a manipulative device used to gain advantages or overcome disadvantages in the society (see Hawkins and Lorinskas, 1969; Bailey and Katz, 1969; Prenti, 1967; and others). Latinismo corresponds very specifically to Cohen's assertion that "one need not be a Marxist in order to recognize the fact that the earning of a livelihood, the struggle for housing, for higher education, and for other benefits, and similar issues constitute an important variable significantly related to ethnicity" (1974:xv).

The overwhelming majority of the study's respondents—32 out of 34—defined the idea of Latino as a political phenomenon.[1] The case of a first-generation Mexican American leader, who worked in the Puerto Rican community of Westtown for over 15 years, represents a classic expression of this sentiment: "Latino is the only way for us to crack the political barrier; to elect our own candidates, to get better schooling for our children, and more and better jobs."

A second-generation Mexican American, who is currently working for the Mexican American Legal Defense and Education Fund (MALDEF), also sees Latinismo as a manifestation of political interests and consciousness. He sees this ethnic group form as a political strategy that can be used to elect officials who would, in turn, serve as models for all Latinos to identify with: "Certainly, one of the biggest problems that we face in Chicago is the lack of role models in politics, academics, and all the professions." A second-generation Puerto Rican community leader flatly describes the concept of Latino or Hispanic as a political strategy. He suggests that Latinismo implies "having one of our own deciding what portion of the pie we are entitled to."

A similar view appears at the base of the Puerto Rican Organization for Political Action (PROPA), an organization established in the early 1970s with the aim of facilitating the development of Spanish-speaking political power in the city of Chicago. At PROPA's first annual banquet this ideological sentiment is clearly stated in the program for that evening's events:

> The voice of the people rumbles with the voice of a LATINO Renaissance. We declare that we now invade the political process (which has in the past excluded us). We take it as a civil right and a human right for the benefit of our community. This Renaissance requires that we HONOR OUR members, that we work together on community issues, that we register our people to vote, and finally that we unite behind LATINO candidates. We invite friends who are not LATINOS to participate in this Renaissance. (1973:2)

In its attempt to rally support for three "Latinos" who were cheated by a realtor when buying homes in the near northwest side of the city, the Latin-American Coalition Against Panic-Peddling also defined the city's Spanish-speaking in Latino or Hispanic terms. A flyer was distributed throughout the Westtown/Humboldt Park community urging residents to attend a meeting which would ultimately result in *"Victoria Para Los Hispanos"* (Victory for Hispanics). The organization proclaimed, as noted in the flyer, "We cannot stop the struggle, we have the political power to make all companies that have cheated Hispanics pay."

The various meanings assigned to the idea or concept of Hispanic or Latino indicate quite clearly that it represents an apparent mechanism to pursue, in some instances, the collective interests of some Spanish-speaking groups. This will then mean that as Spanish-speaking people begin to adopt a consciousness as "Latinos," they appear to represent a distinctive, all-embracing interest-group population. This view is understandable in the light of Glazer and Moynihan's *Beyond the Melting Pot* of 1963, that is, since its publication, it has become axiomatic to perceive ethnic groups as interest populations and/or communities. Despite this similarity it is important to point out the limitations of the Glazer and Moynihan argument on interest-group politics. They viewed minority groups in New York City, primarily blacks and Puerto Ricans, as political interest groups based on the assumption that each minority group creates the same kind of political organization and enters into the same basic political process. In terms of Louis Wirth's (1928) "typology of minority groups," Glazer and Moynihan seem to assume that all minority groups are of either pluralistic or assimilative types and that the goals of assimilation or group pluralism can be sought through the existing institutions and techniques available in society. Conversely, they provide little understanding of minority groups who act out their goals through channels other than the routine political institutions in the society.

A more specific view regarding the linking of the pursuit of interests with ethnic distinctions has been provided by Cohen (1974:xvi-xvii):

> In the course of the organization of economic production, exchange, and distribution, and more particularly through the processes of the division of labor, and the competition for greater share of income between men, a variety of interest groups emerge, whose members have some interests in common. To operate successfully an interest group has to develop basic organizational functions: distinctiveness (some writers call it boundary); communication; authority structure; decision-

> making procedure; ideology; and socialization. . . . But even in the advanced liberal industrial societies there are some structural conditions under which an interest group cannot organize itself on formal lines. . . . The members of interest groups who cannot organize formally will thus tend to make use, though largely unconsciously, of whatever cultural mechanisms are available in order to articulate the organization of their grouping. And it is here, in such situations, that political ethnicity comes into being.

I would modify this argument to take into account those cases where individual Spanish-speaking ethnics acting as interest groups coalesce or merge in contexts in which it is possible for such interests to be pursued via an all-encompassing Latino ethnic frame. In other words, Puerto Ricans and Mexican Americans in Chicago, for instance, share individual economic and political interests, and may stand together as "Latinos" or "Hispanics" as a strategic way to appropriate those which are collectively significant and relevant.

The several conceptual formulations of Latino ethnic behavior noted above further suggest that this kind of group identity and consciousness be seen not only as the product of collective intergroup social relations and/or actions, or as a process created or initiated by the leaders of the various groups, but also as a response to the structural similarities commonly shared by these populations. The structural dimension of Latinismo or Hispanismo pertains to the disadvantaged political and economic status imposed upon the various Spanish-speaking groups by the larger American society's system of inequality. This system of inequality has influenced the rise of a Latino ethnic identity among Puerto Ricans and Mexican Americans in Chicago as these groups have come to share common occupational and educational positions, almost total exclusion from the political system, brutality and injustice by police, and the like. In other words, for Mexican Americans and Puerto Ricans in Chicago certain structural forces involving inequalities and injustice have given rise to particular situational contexts which, in turn, have triggered and intensified the creation and expression of a politicized Latino ethnic-conscious behavior.

In effect, it is particularly in situations involving inequality experienced in common by Puerto Rican and Mexican American groups that Latino ethnic behavior is operative. This is to say that certain situational factors have increasingly come to influence and shape interethnic relations between Mexican Americans and Puerto Ricans, often resulting in the sharing and expression of an inclusive Latino ethnic identification. Conversely, this argument would seem to imply that individual Spanish-speaking group encounters which do not directly involve the status inequalities of this larger population do not result in the affirmation of a Latino ethnic identity and consciousness. These relationships may proceed according to the individual and/or national-cultural identities which the separate groups possess, and thus it can be seen that Latinismo or Hispanismo need not be a relevant factor in all social situations concerning structural conditions and the various Spanish-speaking ethnics.

In sum, the fundamental feature of a politicized Latino ethnic identity is the variable significance of this group consciousness found in the structural social relations effecting Mexican Americans and Puerto Ricans. Latino ethnic-conscious behavior and solidarity may be of critical relevance in some situations, while in others it may be totally irrelevant. From this point of view Spanish-speaking groups should not be perceived as sharing and exhibiting Latino ethnic roles in all of their social relations. In the study of Latino ethnic behavior the unit of analysis has shifted from the isolated or spatially dispersed Puerto Rican and Mexican American ethnic groups and communities defined by their national and cultural contents to Latinismo as a social category, a form of structure, embedded within a larger system of intergroup relations and activities. Behavior that had formerly been regarded as traditional (that of Puerto Ricans and Mexican Americans) may now be seen as taking on a *Latino ethnicity*—a product of interaction and communication processes among these groups in response to their marginal position in the institutional life of the larger American society.

A. Different Forms of Latino Political Consciousness

Not always are the ideological formulations of Latino political consciousness homogenous. First, some of the study's respondents use the "presumable cultural aspects" of an "Hispanic tradition" in their expression of Latino ethnic identification. In this case Mexican Americans, Puerto Ricans, Cubans, Central and South Americans have a consciousness-of-kind as Latinos or Hispanics based on the sharing of the Spanish language.

This cultural-political definition of Latinismo is used by organization leaders who represent traditional-reformist groups. By traditional-reformists I mean those organizations whose programs or tactics rely on the conventional electoral process of creating social change. Table 3 shows the organizations that I categorize as traditional-reformists.

Another group of community organization leaders posits their Latinismo as an identity to which they have an obligation. They see the Latino-conscious person as a participant who directly confronts (via any method including protest) the systems of cultural discrimination and inequality of the larger society. In this case Mexican Americans and Puerto Ricans are often viewed as having or sharing a consciousness about Latinismo because they are the groups who collectively participate in combatting inequality in the larger American scene. In other words, conflict-oriented organizations (as I have classified this group) are more likely to include action-oriented actors and groups in their definition of the Latino group and exclude those who do not participate in direct action. (Table 4 lists the conflict-oriented organizations.)

Tables 3 and 4 are used to illustrate some of the general characteristics most responsible for the variations in defini-

TABLE 3

Traditional-Reformist Organizations

Tactics and Strategies	Leaders: Older Age (First Generation, 1960s and Before)	Ethnic Composition	Leaders: Younger Age (Second Generation, 1960s and Before)	Ethnic Composition
Electoral Process	1. Archdiocesan Latin American Committee	Mexican Amer.	1. League of United Latin American Citizens	Mexican Amer.
	2. Mexican Civic Committee	Mexican Amer.	2. Aspira, Inc. of Ill.	Puerto Rican
	3. American G.I. Forum	Mexican Amer.	3. SER for Jobs	Mexican Amer.
	4. Puerto Rican Congress	Puerto Rican	4. Association House	Puerto Rican
	5. Caballeros de San Juan	Puerto Rican	5. Commonwealth of P.R.	Puerto Rican
	6. Mexican Community Committee of South Chicago	Mexican Amer.		
	7. Latin American Task Force	Mexican Amer.		
	8. Puerto Rican Chamber of Commerce	Puerto Rican		
	9. Puerto Rican Parade Organization	Puerto Rican		
	10. American Spanish Institute	Mixed		

Tactics and Strategies	Leaders: Younger Age (Second Generation, 1970s and After)	Ethnic Composition
Electoral Process	1. Brotherhood against Slavery to Addiction	Mexican Amer.
	2. Latino Youth Alternative High School	Mexican Amer.
	3. Spanish Coalition for Jobs	Mexican Amer.

TABLE 4

Conflict-Oriented Organizations

Tactics and Strategies	Leaders: Older Age (First Generation, 1960s and Before)	Ethnic Composition	Leaders: Younger Age (Second Generation, 1960s and Before)	Ethnic Composition
Confrontation	1. Northwest Employment Development Corporation	Puerto Rican	1. Pilsen Neighbors	Mexican Amer.
	2. Latin American Organization Pro-Action	Puerto Rican	2. Centro Latino/ Universidad	Mixed
	3. Spanish Action Committee of Chicago	Puerto Rican	3. Puerto Rican United Front	Puerto Rican

Tactics and Strategies			Leaders: Younger Age (Second Generation, 1970s and After)	Ethnic Composition
Confrontation			1. Mujeres Latinas En Accion	Mexican Amer.
			2. Mexican American Legal Defense and Educational Fund	Mexican Amer.
			3. Centro Unidad Latina	Puerto Rican
			4. United Neighborhood Organization	Mexican Amer.
			5. Westtown Concerned Citizens Coalition	Puerto Rican

tions and promotion of Latino ethnicity in Chicago. Although one can observe a generational difference between the leaders of the two types of organizations, the "tactics or strategy" variable represents the major significant difference which is intimately related to the organizations' views and expressions of Latino ethnic identity and consciousness. The effect of this variable on the definition of Latinismo will be explained below after examining the two ways that this concept is formulated by the study's respondents.

1. The Cultural-Political Type of Latino Group Identity

To the leaders of the traditional-reformist community organizations Latino ethnic solidarity is determined on the basis of the person's origin and cultural background. In their conceptual formulation of Latino ethnic identity the leaders of the traditional-reformist community organizations subsume all of the Spanish-speaking under a wider Latino category in order to enlarge the group so that it can exert more influence for social, political, and economic progress. For example, in rallying enthusiasm among the various Spanish-speaking groups in the city a first-generation Puerto Rican community leader who used to run a traditional-reformist organization has occasionally viewed this group as having "all of the ingredients to become a major political force in the entire city." One of this respondent's strongest calls for a Latino perspective is reflected in the following quote:

> In Chicago we have all of these groups who can speak Spanish and the truth of the matter is that this may be the factor to bring us together. We need to look into that. There is a great deal of commonality and experience in these groups. This may very well bring us back to Spain. But this also tells us that we have more in common than in differences. In fact, I just came from Israel and we were with this guy who had been there for 18 years—an Israeli from Peru—and his wife was an Israeli from Argentina who had lived there for 23 years. We visited

> their home. It was just like being back home. We eat the same food and drink the same drinks. We were just like brothers and sisters. It was something real. This was heavy, and politically here in Chicago, is the only way to go. Individually, we are not going anywhere. So respect for differences could represent a way for us to unite. The idea of Latinismo is a very good strategy, not only for me but for all Latinos.

This sentiment is also shared by first-generation Mexican Americans who run traditional-reformist organizations. One respondent who has been a resident of the city of Chicago for over twenty years refers to this group consciousness as an "identity that *el pueblo* [the community] has adopted since we are experiencing that we are not only Mexicans, Puerto Ricans, Cubans, Central and South Americans, but we are also Latinos." The same respondent added:

> I feel pity for those leaders that stand up in meetings and say 'we must fight and struggle for the rights of the Puerto Ricans, the Mexicans, or the Cubans separately.' I feel pity for these leaders because they do not understand Latinismo. They do not know that we have basically the same culture and needs. And the only way to alleviate those problems and gain political respect is to work together as one group.

Even some second-generation leaders use the idea of primordiality in the formulation of Latino ethnicity. One such leader from the Pilsen community indicated a preference for the term "Hispanic" over Latino, since the latter includes other people who do not speak Spanish. She defines the former as "being comprised of people of Hispanic ancestry who speak the same language, like the Puerto Ricans, Mexicans, Cubans, and Central and South Americans."

These remarks indicate how the supporters of the cultural-political view attempt to widen the boundaries of the Latino ethnic group to include all of the Spanish-speaking groups. These conceptual forms correspond to the primordial connotation of ethnicity commonly used by some social scientists. This view focuses on the transplanted cultural heritage as the principal antecedent and defining characteristic of ethnic groups. For instance, when responding to the question "Why are commitments to heritage and origin maintained when in terms of other utilitarian values such continued commitment is debilitating?", DeVos (1975) suggests that the answer lies in the surmise that ethnicity in an essential orientation to the past, to collective origin. Celebrated in rituals, narratives, and histories, ethnicity is the sense of belonging, the submersion of the self in something that transcends self, the "we-ness" of heritage and ancestry. In a similar way Devereaux (1975) argues that ethnic boundaries follow as a consequence of commitment to, and identity with, the group. Boundaries are a means of preserving the self-identity, not an end in themselves.

The supporters of the cultural-political view of Latino ethnic identity appear to have adopted a fundamentally cultural approach to define this group form: they chose to elevate one element of culture (the Spanish language) into the main pillar of Latino ethnic identification. The approach of singling out language as the basic defining ingredient of Latino or Hispanic ethnic-conscious identity resembles one of nationalism's abiding myths, defined by Smith (1981:45) as "the identification of nationality with a language." The role of language in nationalism has been emphasized by many scholars, most notably by Boehm (1933), who called it the most important factor in modern nationalism. Although some of what Boehm wrote requires modification, his discussion of language and nationalism can serve the purpose for this comparison:

> The concept of a mother tongue has made language the source from which springs all intellectual and spiritual existence. The mother tongue represents the most suitable expression of spiritual individuality. . . . A people not only transmit the store of all its memories through the vocabulary of its language, but in syntax, word sound and rhythm it finds the most faithful expression of its temperament and general emotional life. . . . The development of a linguistic pluralism such as the Afrikaans

as opposed to the Dutch, the American to the English, the Pennsylvania Dutch or Luxembourgian to High German, is a symptom which reveals, even outside the realm of language, divisions and separations from earlier and more comprehensive social groups. (1933:235)

Indeed, it is language which constitutes, for the proponents of the cultural-political explanation of Latino identity, the chief bond among Mexican Americans, Puerto Ricans, Cubans, and others. For Latinismo or Hispanismo is basically a movement which conceives the natural object of human loyalty to be a fairly large anonymous unit defined by shared language or culture. Thus, there is the tendency to define quite sharply the boundaries of the new emerging Latino identity along linguistic lines.

Correspondingly, one can also suggest that the definition of Latino ethnic identification as a cultural-political strategy clearly reflects on prevailing conceptions of the American political system. It seems to parallel the pluralist notion of American politics so well described by Dahl (1956:145-46): "the normal American process is one in which there is a high probability that an active and legitimate group in the population can make itself heard effectively at some crucial stages in the process of decision." From this perspective the aim of the supporters of the cultural-political view is that this wider and collective "linguistic group" be recognized as a political actor on the national and local levels. This recognition, in turn, would assign to this "Latino community" the tag of another pressure group controlling an "ethnic vote" that can be traded for political concessions.

2. The Sociopolitical Type of Latino Group Identity

Contrary to the primordial or cultural way of defining Latino ethnic identity, leaders of the conflict-oriented community organizations consider as Latinos only those actors and groups who are involved in exerting direct pressures in the form of mass demonstrations, pickets, boycotts, and the like against the larger society's systems of inequality. This sociopolitical construction of Latino ethnic consciousness focuses on treating most Puerto Ricans and Mexican Americans as sharing a Latino consciousness because of their active and direct participation in confronting racism and capital exploitation in urban America. For instance, a second-generation Puerto Rican community leader, whose organization has always been at the forefront of direct confrontation in issues concerning the Spanish-speaking, said: "When we talk about a Latino group identity or coalition in Chicago, it should be built and applied to by the people who come forward and identify themselves."

Similarly, another second-generation Puerto Rican community organization leader defines Latinos more stringently as "only those involved in the issues and not those who emerge as Latinos overnight when something is going to be given to the community." This respondent adds that Puerto Ricans and Mexican Americans are responsible for the "wheeling and dealing or doing political maneuvering, and yet they continue in the same socioeconomic position in comparison to the parent generation."

Second-generation Mexican American community organization leaders also define the idea of a Latino ethnic consciousness as the collective identity of Mexican Americans and Puerto Ricans. One such Mexican American leader describes the idea of Latino as part of a developmental process whereby Boricuas [Puerto Ricans] and Chicanos [Mexican Americans] have come to grips with their own heritage: "I think that the initial points were getting involved in our own identities. What I'm saying is that before we accepted the Latino, we accepted the Chicano, we accepted the Boricua. We accepted ourselves first and Latino second." The same respondent warned, however, that:

> . . . we need to be concerned with the term Latino or Hispanic because that includes everybody. It includes the Cubans, the Central and South Americans, and I have always felt that the struggle has been a Chicano-Boricua struggle. I

> have worked with the city in other capacities and I've always seen how they like to impose upon us a Cuban or a South American in positions of power to keep the Chicanos and Boricuas divided.

Another second-generation Mexican American, and a leader of a traditional-reformist organization, advances the categorization of a Puerto Rican and Mexican American type of Latino ethnicity. Using a conflict-oriented perspective, the respondent said:

> I think that Mexican Americans and Puerto Ricans are the two major groups encompassing the Hispanics in the United States. We are the targets of programs such as Affirmative Action because we are so severely disadvantaged. We are low income, we live in poverty, we attend the worst schools; in general, we seen to adhere to the symbols of Basqueness; and the symbols ent in the United States for so long and they have experienced discrimination and we are the targets of programs that try to resolve this disadvantage. The Cubans who came here have all the tools to make it. And they pass this advantage on to their kids almost guaranteed, just like poverty is guaranteed to be passed on to our kids. So from that point of view the Cubans are not the target group, they are not disadvantaged, they are not discriminated against. The Hispanic is low income and severely disadvantaged.

These views suggest that Latino identity and solidarity are the social product of those groups directly involved in the pursuit of collective goals, advantages, and gains. Unlike the traditional-reformist leaders who define the idea of Latino as a primordial or cultural phenomenon subsuming all of Chicago's Spanish-speaking groups within one wider Latino unit, conflict-oriented leaders see the Latino-conscious person as the "fruit" or outcome of a highly self-conscious, creative process.

The perspective of the proponents of the social-political interpretation of Latino ethnic identity corresponds to the view of several scholars, perhaps most notably Frederick Barth (1969:10), who argues that ethnic groups arise and persist by virtue of "boundary creation and maintenance," that is, social processes that members of the group consciously and actively participate in and help to determine. In Barth's perspective the social "insignia" or "markers" of the ethnic groups are not necessarily elaborate, pervasive, or frequently observed in the group's social life. Typically, in fact, the maintenance of ethnic boundaries is accomplished by "signs, icons, totems" and other markings of limited scale, their only function being to distinguish the group in question from other ethnic groups that bound it spatially or temporarily.

The social-political definition of Latino ethnic solidarity parallels the more common interpretation of nationalism which argues that nationalists are those who struggle for the liberation or independence of one's state. Heiberg (1979: 195-96) provides an example by defining "Basques" as persons who "fight" for the liberation of this group identity:

> For political purposes a Basque—or, rather, a true Basque—is one who actively and politically defines [the] symbols of Basque cohesion and differentiation. The immoral are those who threaten or go against their moral prescriptions. Ethnic assignation—who is or is not considered Basque—is not determined by criteria of descent. . . . A person is "Basque" when he is seen to adhere to the symbols of Basqueness; and the sybols of Basqueness are exclusively nationalist property, a point with which many would violently disagree.

B. Reasons for the Two Forms of Latino Political Consciousness

There are several explanations for the assignment of the cultural- and social-political definitions to Latino or Hispanic ethnic identity. One explanation is directly related to the social position or base of the organizations in the larger society. In other words, this study argues for a theoretical understanding of the ideological sentiments and expressions of the community organizations as given and conditioned by their social position in society. It follows Daherendorf's statement that "the individual who assumes a position in an association finds these role interests with his position, just as he finds certain role expectations from the point of view of the social system" (1959:178). Although community organizations are not "individuals" or "persons," an analogy can be made to suggest that they can be considered as occupying certain positions in society.

There are several indicators that can be used to measure an organization's social position or standing; its funding sources, the prestige afforded by its advisory board membership, its tactics and strategies, and the like. In the absence of a systematic body of empirical data or research in this area, I shall try to sketch and evaluate the relative merit of some alternative model. The starting point is the knowledge or understanding of the strategies or tactics employed by the various organizations in pursuit of their goals and objectives. Therefore, my argument advances that an organization's social base can be partially determined by how or to what extent its tactics, strategies, or ideologies reflect those of the wider society. For example, the electoral tactic or traditional-reformist organizations—a tactic which commonly conforms with the society's ideological base—would place these groups in positions and standings higher than the conflict-oriented groups that rely on confrontational tactics. Confrontation approaches often run counter to the society's way of doing things. From this perspective the two groups' conceptual formulations of Latino ethnic identity and consciousness can be said to be influenced by the social base that they occupy in the larger American society.

Myrdal (1944) used a similar theoretical approach to analyze the controversy among black leaders between "accommodation" and "protest" as alternative strategies for dealing with the host society. He viewed the two styles as being more or less implied by the position of any ethnic group in American society: "they are it, but not wholly of it. They are shaped by the realities of the American polity, a society in which any interest group might alternate between protest and accommodation in trying to further its interests, or divide between protest and accommodationist styles and segments at any given time in advancing its interests" (Myrdal, 1944:779).

Another explanation for the different forms of Latino or Hispanic identity suggested by the various community leaders can be given by examining the "inclusion" and "exclusion," or the "we/they," principles implied in both definitions. Within the cultural-political view the boundary-defining forms of social organization are predicated especially on the language factor, through which membership is ascribed, and is ascribed by others. As indicated earlier, in this formulation the language factor is accorded primacy in organizing the Latino or Hispanic identity; it supplies or provides reference to group orientation. This point is analogous to the one advanced by Barth (1969:13-14):

> A categorical ascription is an ethnic ascription when it classifies a person in terms of his basic, most general identity, presumptively determined by his origin and background. To the extent that actors use ethnic identities to categorize themselves and others for purposes of interaction, they form ethnic groups in this organizational sense.

From this point of view Latino identity is an ascribed or self-ascribed device that socially locates an individual with reference to language similarity. The Spanish language represents an ever-present feature of the process of interaction of those individuals labeled as "Latinos" by the proponents of the cultural-political dimension of Latinismo. In other words, language has become for some Spanish-speaking a primary bond of social cohesion as they take on a wider Latino group identity. The distinction made here is between "Hispanics" or "Latinos" and the wider American society or simply non-Spanish-speaking groups.

Within the social-political dimension of the Latino ethnic identity, on the other hand, the boundaries of this wider collectivity are situationally selected. A central assumption underlying this view is that since there are several identifications which Spanish-speaking persons can apply to themselves, the significant question is not who are the "Latinos" or "Hispanics," but rather when and how and why the identification Latino or Hispanic is preferred. From such a perspective membership in the Latino category attributes to members some expectations as to how they are to behave, the patterns of activity that they will engage in, the resources and rewards to be gained from this intergroup relationship, and the interests to be protected. For the proponents of the social-political view, then, the Latino ethnic category provides members with the elements of a "corporate history" in time and space: a history which offers some explanation for their collective membership as "Latinos," why they are members, where they originated, and why the existence of the Latino identification is substantial and legitimate. Viewed somewhat differently, for this group of leaders the Latino ethnic identification provides Spanish-speaking persons with the elements of a "social biography" which connects their cultural and structural similarities with social behavior. A similar observation is made by Greenwood (1973), who suggests that as the "Basque" ethnic category began to be differentiated from that of "Spaniards" in seventeenth-century Spain, the former claimed that they "were the first inhabitants of the peninsula after the Universal Flood and that their culture and collective nobility arose from time immemorial (before the existence of the Spanish crown)." From this point of view the Latino or Hispanic membership provides certain Spanish-speaking persons with an historical base or framework which they use to orient themselves to other Spanish-speakers, either as fellow members or as "other kinds" of people.

As a whole, for both proponents of the cultural-spare and the social-political definitions of Latinismo what stands out are the frustrations, the dilemmas, and above all the powerlessness afflicting traditional-reformists and conflict-oriented groups alike. For this collectivity of leaders, whose constituencies grow more diverse as their numerical power increases, both strategies—tradition-reformist and conflict-oriented—become dimensions of the political process. And although there exists what appears to be a wide variance in the conceptual meanings assigned to Latino ethnic behavior, we can still suggest that when we look at the two ideological formulations (e.g., one fired by an ideology which puts a premium on language solidarity or one based on a perception of being victimized by systems of racial or cultural inequality), the leaders of the Spanish-speaking communities are seeking to ensure that their demands are met by society's major institutions and structures. In short, the social organization of traditional-reformist and conflict-oriented groups represents an attempt to alter existing social and power arrangements between the Spanish-speaking and the larger American social structure.

Further, there is at least one other major element implied in the presentation of these definitional forms of the concept of Latino or Hispanic. Perceiving the minimal existence of Latino identity as the organization of interacting poor and oppressive Spanish-speaking ethnics, on the one hand, or as the identity of a linguistic group, on the other hand, highlights the need to know what contrastive ethnic categories are operative in a given place at a given time. In other words, I argue that knowledge of the concept of Latino or Hispanic cannot be dismissed simply by stating, as Cohen (1974:x) does, that "what matters sociologically is what people actually do, not what they subjectively think or what they think they think." Moreover, knowledge of the Latino ethnic category also implies information about the range of people that can be viewed as constituting this wider and collective group form. Therefore, the different ideological sentiments expressed by the study's respondents highlight the differential composition and organization of Latino ethnic membership sets in different places and as seen from different viewpoints of membership. The crucial fact remains that the contrastive definitions of Latinismo or Hispanismo exist and are expressed in particular ways. Without this basis there is little point in trying to demonstrate what matters "sociologically" in terms of the concept of Latino or Hispanic if the contrastive ideological sentiments of members of this category have not been delineated.

3

Latino Ethnic Mobilization:

The Spanish Coalition for Jobs

AFFIRMATIVE ACTION

"Ethnic mobilization is," according to Professor Olzak (1983:355), "the process by which groups organize around some feature of ethnic identity (for example, skin color, language, customs) in pursuit of collective ends." From this point of view Latino ethnic mobilization can be said to represent the collective action—action of two or more Spanish-speaking groups as opposed to the mobilization of individual Spanish-speaking ethnics—that take a language identification as criterion for membership. Certain external stimuli serve to excite identification with this language group into Latino ethnic mobilization.

The leading factor responsible for stirring Latino ethnic mobilization among Puerto Ricans and Mexican Americans in Chicago during the early 1970s was the Affirmative Action policy. The Affirmative Action policy represented the instrument or mechanism used by leaders from the two communities to make claims against institutions and structures found to be discriminating against Spanish-speaking workers at the citywide level. Viewed another way, the Affirmative Action policy provided the critical base for the Mexican

American and Puerto Rican leadership to advance the interests of their populations collectively rather than as individual or separate Spanish-speaking ethnics. It enabled ununited groups to transcend the boundaries of their individual ethnic groups and assert demands as a Latino population or group.

The idea of Affirmative Action was incorporated into the Civil Rights Act of 1964. This act banned discrimination in voting, in places of public accommodation, in public facilities, federal programs, federally supported public education, and employment; and it created an Equal Employment Opportunity Commission to enforce the ban on discrimination in employment because of the individual's race, color, religion, sex, or national origin. The words "affirmative action" occur in one place in the act, section 706(g): "If the court finds that the respondent has intentionally engaged in or is intentionally engaging in an unlawful practice charged in the complaint, the court may enjoin the respondent from engaging in such unlawful employment practice, and order such affirmative action as may be appropriate" (Federal Civil Rights Enforcement Effort, 1973). Further, Title VI provides for the termination of federal funds from any state or local program administered in a discriminatory manner. For instance, Executive Order 11246, issued by President Johnson in 1965, requires all federal contractors to take "affirmative action" in the hiring of minorities. In addition, this executive order extended Affirmative Action to all private contractors, subcontractors, and unions dealing with the federal government (Federal Civil Rights Enforcement Effort, 1973).

That the Affirmative Action policy was of great importance for the organization, development, and growth of a Latino identity and agenda is clearly reflected in a memo sent by the chair of one community organization in the Puerto Rican *barrio* to social service agencies and officials in the Spanish-speaking communities of the city during the spring of 1971. In it attention was called to the "full rights of citizens from Latin America, including the protection of the government against the dehumanizing conditions of Latinos" (Acute Depression in the Latin American Community, 1971:1). In the same memo the two leading priorities of the "Latino community" were specifically directed at the implementation of the Affirmative Action policy by all employers (1971:1):

(1) All federal agencies, state and private, which administer federal funds, be compelled to adhere to the 1964 and 1968 Civil Rights Statutes and other federal laws to hire Latinos at all levels with direct federal criteria for enforcement;

(2) In the enforcement of full rights of American citizenship according to the U.S. Constitution and Federal Statutes—that all Affirmative Action plans filed by private companies be made public record. That a doctrine of community participation in the processing and implementation of the Affirmative Action plan of particular interest to us Latinos—be a federal requirement for compliance.

The importance of the Affirmative Action policy to the development and growth of a Latino identity and mobilization was also expressed in an interview by the present executive director of the Spanish Coalition for Jobs (a discussion on this organization will soon follow):

> . . . the Spanish Coalition for Jobs started because of Affirmative Action. This was in the early 1970's when a group of Hispanic Manpower Service agencies throughout the city of Chicago became concerned mostly with the utility companies and major chain stores where we did not see Hispanics or our brown faces working there. The courts were not implementing the Affirmative Action policy as it applied to Latinos: however, the act was there to be used and force employers to carry it out. So Affirmative Action gave birth to the Spanish Coalition.

In the same interview she added: "We needed no longer to theorize and speculate on the matter of job discrimination. We knew that equal employment opportunity could be significantly advanced via the provisions of Affirmative Action."

Fundamentally, the Affirmative Action policy provided Puerto Rican and Mexican American leaders the legal sanction from which to seek meaningful responses and resolution to the various grievances of Spanish-speaking people in general. Opening doors long closed was a necessary first step; making sure that those who were formerly locked out had a real opportunity to compete—that is, not only to enter but also to move upward—was the thrust of the Mexican American and Puerto Rican leadership. Affirmative Action was the key to achieving these goals.

The analysis of the influence of social programs and/or policies such as Affirmative Action on the emergence and growth of a group consciousness has relevance in a comparative context in light of Thomas Plau's (1969:18-19) suggestions about the role of the Community Action Programs in the War on Poverty policy that were legislated during the 1960s from proposals out of the Office of Economic Opportunity. He pointed out the principal outcomes of these programs:

> What community action has done is to encourage a political consciousness among the poor, and is thus more important for what it has done for its supporters themselves than for what goals it has gained for them. . . . It has encouraged the desire to have some control over problems and bureaucracies that have barricaded themselves in against people that they are supposed to be serving.

The fact that big-city mayors wanted and were eventually able to curb the influence of Community Action Programs is further evidence of the politicizing and mobilizing effect which the programs had upon the urban poor. According to Silberman's (1969:85) discussion, the following is an example of the way these programs were viewed:

> What the mayors fear, in effect is another large redistribution of political power in the cities. Their own power has been associated with the growth of the welfare state since the 1930's, which has meant a vast funneling of federal, state, and local money through their offices. Now, the mayors perceive [that] the war on poverty may bring about another shift in which the poor would look to Washington or to their own organizations. Either way, they would be less amenable to the influence of City Hall.

Indeed, a considerable number of poor people benefited from participation in the Community Action Programs. Community Action Programs also helped to raise the expectations of the poor and provided a valuable organizational and political education for their participants, whose skills were often later put to use in other organizations. As Rubin (1967:14) has commented, the poor were "called upon to speak in their behalf, to assess their needs," and they gained a new confidence "in the efficacy of organization to correct the gnawing grievances that plague their lives."

In the same vein the Affirmative Action policy certainly helped spur the organization of a Latino ethnic agenda or program in Chicago. The Affirmative Action policy legitimized the claims made by Puerto Ricans and Mexican Americans in the collective. It served as the instrument by which these claims could be advanced by Spanish-speaking organizations to mobilize their members under a "Latino ethnic identity" and use the strength of a larger numerical group to force those institutions that discriminated against the Spanish-speaking to implement the Affirmative Action policy. Viewed differently, the presence of availability of a legal statute encouraged the collective organization of groups which traditionally had focused primarily on resolving the problems of their individual population without transcending these boundaries. In the remainder of the chapter we will examine one case of Latino ethnic mobilization in Chicago.

THE SPANISH COALITION FOR JOBS

There is evidence that a Latino ethnic group identity and consciousness among Mexican American and Puerto Rican community organizations in Chicago began to emerge in the early 1970s.[1] In recognition of the frustration and anger of the Spanish-speaking working class because of this population's marginal participation in the American economy as well as subjection to discrimination by American firms, a coalition of various Puerto Rican and Mexican American community organizations was formed in June 1971 to alleviate these conditions. The Spanish Coalition for Jobs (La Coalicion Latinoamericana de Empleos, as this coalition was named) was formed primarily as a response to the marginal integration of Spanish-speaking workers in the labor force in American industries and corporations such as Illinois Bell Telephone and Jewel Tea.

A proposal to the Rockefeller Foundation (1972) indicates that the Spanish Coalition for Jobs, as an organization of organizations (a protest-type coalition), was comprised of 23 Puerto Rican and Mexican American local community organizations, including nine employment referral agencies from the Pilsen, South Chicago, Lakeview, and Westtown/Humboldt Park communities. The roots of the Spanish Coalition for Jobs are found in the issue of employment, namely, job discrimination. The organization's involvement in job discrimination cases started when several employment agencies came to recognize that a large number of their Spanish-speaking referrals to large American firms were not being placed in jobs. This concern was expressed in one of the Spanish Coalition's reports: "Employers were giving two or three token jobs to the referral agencies to satisfy them, but very few of these companies ever considered hiring significant numbers of Latinos. . . . as consumers we were welcomed, but as candidates for jobs we were being ignored" ("History of the Spanish Coalition for Jobs"). The influence of job discrimination upon the creation of a Latino ethnic identity is also described in the proposal to the Rockefeller Foundation noted above: "the racist attitude of employers triggered us into utilizing our consumer power as a tool or bargaining device . . . to compete in the job market" (1972).

The Spanish Coalition for Jobs typifies one particular case of a citywide group representing the interests of a multiethnic and powerless population. Additionally, it can be considered Chicago's first Latino protest organization, that is, an organization comprised of more than one Spanish-speaking group which employed protest tactics to achieve its programs and goals. Protest represented to the Spanish Coalition for Jobs the most feasible mechanism to acquire political influence. The organization lacked the political resources to bargain with decision-makers to promote the interests of their constituents. It represented a case of an organization which had to rely on the power of numbers and resort to protest in order to achieve responsiveness to constituency concerns.

As a protest organization the Spanish Coalition for Jobs had the advantage of relying on existing local community organizations and agencies as one part of the organization's constituency. Its other segment was the mass-based membership of these groups. These local community groups were especially critical for the Spanish Coalition's rapid growth since it did not have to create them from the very beginning. The importance of existing community groups in the formative process of organizations is shown in Fish's (1971) analysis of The Woodlawn Organization (T.W.O.) in Chicago. He observed that many "civic-minded groups were present in Woodlawn, but they lacked either support or the clout to deal effectively with the problems Woodlawn faced" (1971:16).

T.W.O.'s and the Spanish Coalition for Jobs' relationships with existing institutions are rooted in Saul Alinsky's theory of community organization, which emphasizes the value of building on existing social ties: "the foundation of a People's Organization is the communal life of people. . . . [in] the building of a People's Organization, the agencies and local traditions are, to an important extent, the flesh and blood of the community." In other words, "community organizers must work with all of the agencies of the community to build a People's Organization of which they [the agencies] are the very foundation" (Alinsky, 1969:76).

The importance of the various Puerto Rican and Mexican American community organizations to the development of the Spanish Coalition for Jobs can be measured in the institutional strength that they represented. The social networks institutionalized by the existing community groups (the organizations' mass-based membership), as well as the local leadership within them, were a vital resource for the coalition. More specifically, the community organizations and agencies, by providing services and programs to residents of a particular neighborhood, established regular contacts with their clients. And since the most important resource for a protest-oriented organization like the Spanish Coalition for Jobs is numbers (Lipsky, 1971), its ability to accomplish desired resolutions of issues depended on how many people it was able to turn out for meetings and actions. The existing community organizations provided the coalition with an established mass-based constituency.

Another role played by the different local community organizations and agencies was the contribution they could make to support the efforts of the coalition, since the latter was strictly a volunteer organization. Not having funds to operate, the different groups provided staff, meeting space, and other resources crucial for the development of the organization. Conversely, as an organization of organizations, the Spanish Coalition for Jobs offered its member organizations an important incentive that the organizations by themselves did not possess: the utility of cooperative action for solving certain problems experienced by the different Puerto Rican and Mexican American populations.

Wilson (1973:31), who developed the notion of "purposive incentives," defined incentives as "any valued benefits, service, or opportunity, in exchange for which an individual is willing to contribute time, effort, or resources to an organization," and receive an adequate supply of incentives as critical to organizational maintenance. He then distinguished the four categories of organization incentives: (1) material— "tangible rewards: money or things and services readily priced in monetary terms"; (2) collective solidarity— "intangible rewards arising out of the act of associating that must be enjoyed by a group if they are to be enjoyed by anyone . . . involve the fun and conviviality of coming together, the sense of group membership or exclusiveness, and such collective status or esteem as the group as a whole may enjoy"; (3) specific solidarity—"intangible rewards arising out of the act of associating that can be given to, or withheld from specific individuals"; and (4) purposive—"depend crucially on the stated objectives of the organization and are general in that any member of such a group can derive some satisfaction from group efforts even if he himself contributed nothing but his name."

In view of Wilson's scheme the major incentive that the Spanish Coalition for Jobs offered its constituents was to join a Latino organization (collective solidarity) comprised of Mexican American and Puerto Rican organizations to resolve problems that each group separately had been unable to alleviate. Organized to solve the problems of individual Mexican American or Puerto Rican community residents, the local community organizations and agencies had found themselves frequently incapable of securing necessary gains and concessions from American institutions. The argument that the cooperative efforts of an organization of organizations would be more effective than the activities of an individual group was thus a particularly compelling incentive for the local community organizations and agencies.

A. Illinois Bell

Although the Spanish Coalition for Jobs could depend on the network of the existing community organizations and agencies, it needed an "event, issue or threat" to mobilize its mass base as a "Latino collectivity." That is, having the support of the established organizations and their constituents was not sufficient to excite political action or mobilization as one Latino unit. The coalition's mass-based membership had to be convinced that "functioning as Latinos" during those situational contexts when certain issues affected them similarly would be more advantageous than approaching them from the vantage point of individual Mexican American or Puerto Rican organizations.

Mollenkopf (1973:9), in a comparative study of community organizations, found that issues "involving a clear collective bad for some groups were most effective in mobilizing communities." Wilson (1972:203), generalizing from several case studies, concluded that:

> . . . there must be belief among the members of a potential organization that matters of concern to them are being affected by other institutions in a society whose behavior can be altered. That belief is more likely to emerge when a highly visible person or organization appears to be posing a serious threat to some value of importance to the potential members.

For the Spanish Coalition for Jobs' mass-based membership, however, this belief had to be developed; it would not simply "emerge." In an interview one of the study's respondents stated that "people in the community were all aware that their interests were being affected by outside institutions, but their experiences had also promoted a feeling that there was nothing they could do to change this system." Thus, the Spanish Coalition for Jobs not only had to emphasize the presence of a "threat" (in this case an issue) but also had to demonstrate to its mass base that they could affect the issue collectively as one Latino group.

The source of this approach to interpreting community problems lies in the work of Alinsky (1972:105): "if people feel they don't have the power to change a bad situation, then they do not think about it." He also said, "an issue is something you can do something about, but as long as you feel powerless and unable to do anything about it, all you have is a bad scene" (1972:105).

In the case of the Spanish Coalition for Jobs the issue—job discrimination against Latino workers by Illinois Bell—was clearly present, since Spanish-speaking referrals to this company, as members of the coalition had noted, were seldom placed in jobs. As the director of the Spanish Coalition for Jobs informed me in one interview:

> We started to make contact with the person who was in charge of public relations at Illinois Bell. We would meet with that person regularly and tell him what our concerns were. Instead, he would try to play games with us by telling us that they did not discriminate against any people, that they take people based on qualifications. We would then say to him, "you mean to tell us that in the entire city of Chicago you cannot find one Latino for your company?" Or, we would say, "you mean to tell us that all the applicants that we refer to you are not, even one, qualified for your company?"

Further, according to a memorandum titled "Acute Depression in the Latin American Community" issued in the spring of 1971, member organizations of the Spanish Coalition had disclosed that out of Illinois Bell's 44,000 employees, fewer than 300 were Latinos.

Thus, given the existence of an issue, what was necessary for the Spanish Coalition for Jobs to mobilize the various Spanish-speaking populations around a Latino group identity was an event which would demonstrate the ability of a "Latino group" to influence the agency from which that issue originated. The event was provided during a community meeting on August 5, 1971, at the Association House in Westtown. The meeting was called by Illinois Bell officials to discuss the different services that the telephone company was offering its "Spanish-speaking customers." One Illinois Bell official openly declared to the audience that his corporation had not always readily employed Spanish-speaking workers in the past. Several representatives of the Spanish Coalition, among many in attendance, used this moment to inform the 300 people present that Illinois Bell had a history of discriminating against Latino workers. A description by one of my respondents of what took place that night gives us an insight as to why the meeting became almost a forum of protest:

> I had heard about the meeting with the Illinois Bell people at the Association House because my son was the director there at the time. Illinois Bell wanted to give us a show about the things that they were doing to improve services to the Latinos. Other people who had heard about the meeting started talking about doing something against the telephone company for not respecting us. I mean, we would send people to be interviewed there and they were never interviewed. And then the people from Illinois Bell would tell us that our people did not show up. So we decided that during the meeting at the Association House we would ask them, instead, about jobs.

Although very little material benefits were gained from the meeting, the Spanish Coalition for Jobs won a symbolic victory. The representatives of the telephone company agreed to an initial negotiation meeting to discuss the job issue with the members of the Spanish Coalition for Jobs.

Between the August 5th meeting at Association House and the subsequent meeting with telephone company officials the members of the Spanish Coalition for Jobs met several times to discuss strategies for the event. It was agreed to develop a list of demands to present at the next meeting with the utility company officials. On August 17, 1971, the members of the Spanish Coalition met to construct this list. One of the coalition's monthly reports (1971:1) indicates that a committee of 10 persons was appointed to speak for the group and present the following demands:

(1) 3,000 jobs over a period of three years;
(2) appointment of a Latino Review Committee;
(3) appointment of a liaison person to work with the Latino community and Illinois Bell;
(4) establishment of a training center in Westtown; and
(5) 30 percent of their funds for contributions to organizations to be allocated to the Spanish community.

The first formal meeting between the two groups was finally held September 15, 1971, at the Association House. The negotiation session was attended by Illinois Bell's manager of urban affairs, the assistant vice president in charge of personnel, and a Spanish-speaking staff member; members of the Spanish Coalition for Jobs; and 200 community residents. According to a *Sun-Times* report (1971:13), after the Spanish Coalition for Jobs' list of demands was presented, the company's assistant vice president offered 115 jobs for the Spanish community, after stating that the other demands could not be met. The same report alluded to the contradictions in the vice president's statements, since refusal to meet the Coalition's demands was made after an acknowledgment that the "telephone company was in need of more bilingual workers" (1971:13).

The coalition's representatives refused the telephone company's offer and the following day conducted its first mass demonstration as a "Latino collectivity" at the Illinois Bell office at 712 West Washington Street near downtown Chicago. One of the local community newspapers reported that some 100 members of the Spanish Coalition, who accused the telephone company of discriminating against Latinos, "first marched outside the company's employment office, then about 50 of them moved into the first-floor employment office, where six filled out job application forms" (*Booster*, 1972:1).

This exchange of negotiations followed by protest tactics is indicative of the yearlong adverse relationship between the Spanish Coalition and the Illinois Bell Telephone Company. Basically, there would be negotiations; and when those broke down, picketing would begin of Illinois Bell officials' and executives' homes by members of the Spanish Coalition.

Finally, on June 14, 1972, the Illinois Bell Telephone Company signed an agreement with the Spanish Coalition for Jobs. Under the terms of the agreement it was expected that Illinois Bell would hire at least 1,323 Latinos by the end of 1976, including two top-level executives (*Booster*,

1972:2). The promise of 1,323 additional Spanish-speaking workers was virtually a fulfillment of the Spanish Coalition's main demand. The *Booster* (1972:3) further reported that the Spanish Coalition was pleased "with a provision in the eight-point agreement calling for regular review by the Coalition of the company's progress toward achieving its hiring goals."

B. Jewel Tea Company

In order to sustain the Spanish Coalition for Jobs as a protest organization representing the collective interests of Mexican Americans and Puerto Ricans under a Latino group category, it became necessary for the organization to work on several issues affecting both groups. The approach of "interrelationship of issues" is fundamentally basic to the Alinsky philosophy of community organizing on which the Spanish Coalition for Jobs was founded. Alinsky's (1969:60) discussion of building "People's Organizations" stressed the interrelationship of problems and the maintenance value of many issues:

> The conventional community council—which means practically all community councils—soon discovers that the problems of life are not wrapped up in individual cellophane packages, and because the community council cannot and does not want to get down to the roots of the problems, it retreats into a sphere of trivial, superficial ameliorations. The people judge the agency by its programs and soon define the agency as insignificant.
>
> The program of a real People's Organization calmly accepts the overwhelming fact that all problems are related and that they are all progeny of certain fundamental causes, that ultimate success in conquering these evils can be achieved only by victory over all evils.

Alinsky later, in *Rules for Radicals* (1972:120), expanded this point:

> Organizations must be based on many issues. Organizations need action as an individual needs oxygen. The cessation of

> action brings death to the organization through factionalism and inaction, through dialogues and conferences that are actually a form of rigor mortis rather than life. It is impossible to maintain constant action on a single issue. A single issue is a fatal straitjacket that will stifle the life of an organization. Furthermore, a single issue drastically limits your appeal, where multiple issues would draw in the many potential members essential to the building of a broad, mass-based organization.

Alinsky's analysis, then, suggestive of one way in which a multiplicity of issues can promote organizational survival: when one issue is resolved, the presence of another one provides a reason for continued involvement. Or as suggested by Wilson (1973:30), "the effect to a multi-issue approach served in two ways toward producing and sustaining cooperative efforts."

In keeping with the Alinsky model, the Jewel Tea Company became the coalition's second target of confrontation for discrimination against Spanish-speaking workers. The Jewel controversy started even before the Illinois Bell issue had been completely resolved: the leadership of the Spanish Coalition decided to pursue another issue immediately after the telephone company agreed to meet their demands. The Spanish Coalition for Jobs began its relationship with the food company chain from a "bargaining" position rather than with the protest tactics employed against its first target.

One possible explanation for the shift in tactics is found in Alinsky and Lipsky, who stress that an organization must continually develop new tactics in order to maximize the adversary's vulnerability, gain publicity, and thus effectiveness. According to Alinsky (1972:163), "once a specific tactic is used, it ceases to be outside the experience of the enemy. Before long, he devises counter-measures that void the previously effective tactic." Or as Lipsky (1970:131) observed, "protest leaders must continually develop new dramatic techniques in order to receive their life-blood or publicity: [a tactic] which has been used before is unlikely to be deemed newsworthy, and the lack of media attention diminishes the chances of success." In sum, both argue that new tactics must therefore be developed in order to make the opposition vulnerable.

Another partial explanation can be derived from Wilson's (1973:282) view that protest is a means of acquiring bargaining resources. When resources for bargaining have been acquired, protest is no longer necessary—the organizations can negotiate with target institutions.

By the time the Jewel issue emerged, the Spanish Coalition for Jobs seemed to have been halfway down the road from protest to negotiation. It had not yet achieved the regularized access to public and private officials necessary for a bargaining relationship; however, it was assumed that the protest tactics employed against Illinois Bell demonstrated the legitimacy of the organization's grievances, so that it was no longer necessary to dramatize an issue in order to gain a hearing from targets. As one of the coalition's organizers during that period informed me in an interview, "the coalition received the recognition that made it a respected organization. People in government and in private business were taking a serious look at us."

According to the report "Joint Venture Agreement: Spanish Coalition for Jobs and Jewel" (1972:1) the coalition began negotiations with Jewel Tea officials in February 1972 for "the purpose of mutual exploration of Jewel's hiring policies and plan to hire Latinos in Cook County." Basically, the same agreement for jobs which Illinois Bell and the Spanish Coalition signed June 14, 1972, was the basis for the negotiations between the two groups. In a news release dated August 9, 1972, the coalition's proposal to Jewel was made public; it called for 600 full-time and 1,300 part-time jobs for Spanish-speaking workers.

The major reason the Spanish Coalition for Jobs made Jewel its next target of confrontation was primarily because of some findings concerning the company's hiring practice of Spanish-speaking workers. Again, several of the coalition's member organizations disclosed Jewel's racist hiring practices. For instance, it was reported in a news release by the coalition (1972:2) that out of a work force of 6,000 full-time workers, only 86 were Latinos, and from 13,000 part-timers, only 151 were Latinos. The news release also stated that the food company chain had received over a quarter of a million dollars from the federal government to train minorities, and only 140 Latinos had received training up to that date.

In March 1972 members of the Spanish Coalition for Jobs met for the first time with representatives from Jewel. The major demands presented to Jewel officials were: "(1) a job training program for Latinos, (2) an increase of Latino workers, (3) the hiring of Latinos to administrative positions, and (4) a greater increase in participation by community residents in the supervising of how Latinos are being processed" (*El Informador Newspaper*, 1973:3). These negotiations broke down after several hours of bargaining when the Jewel officials rejected the Spanish Coalition's demands. In another news release the coalition called the Jewel response to their demands a "rejection of the Latino community and a callous lack of corporate responsibility to the community."

As indicated earlier, the tactics that were employed against Illinois Bell were not repeated by the Spanish Coalition for Jobs in its dealings with Jewel; and it was not until an entire year had elapsed of bargaining negotiations with the food chain's officials that the coalition resorted to protest as a way to secure perquisites for its constituents. The coalition's first mass demonstration, in the form of a boycott against Jewel, began Saturday, April 13, 1973, at 9:00 A.M. A local community newspaper reported that "members from the Spanish Coalition for Jobs met at the front of Jewel's 14 stores for several hours distributing leaflets and urging shoppers not to buy at Jewel" (*El Informador Newspaper*, 1973:3). The same source noted that the positive reaction of the shoppers could be measured by the large number who boycotted the supermarkets. It was also indicated that the real test and effect of the boycott occurred the following day when the Jewel store located on Damen and North (in the Puerto Rican community of Westtown) closed down at 3:00 P.M. because people refused to shop at the store.

After several months of picketing and shoppers' boycotting of Jewel stores in the Spanish-speaking barrios, Jewel signed an agreement with the Spanish Coalition for Jobs late in the summer of 1973. The agreement called for 50 job-training positions, and while Jewel provided the on-the-job training as part of the arrangement, it was further agreed that the "Northwest Employment Development Corporation, acting in behalf of the Spanish Coalition for Jobs, would supervise the implementation of the program as well as provide supportive services" (*El Informador Newspaper*, 1973:1). The jobs allocated for Latinos were: 10 clerical (office), 10 clerical (store), 5 meat packing, 5 product pricing, 5 truck drivers, 5 forklift operators, 5 stockroom clerks, and 5 inventory control.

In sum, the Illinois Bell and Jewel controversies provided both material and symbolic benefits to the Spanish Coalition constituency. The job-opening and job-training agreements secured from the two companies by the Spanish Coalition are clearly material, for the ability to secure employment or a better-paying job improves the economic position of individual beneficiaries. The individual economic gains also indirectly contribute to community stability, in the form of increased financial support for local businesses, to cite one example.

On a more symbolic level, these successes demonstrated that adoption of a "Latino ethnic identity" could alter institutional racist practices, and thus contributed to the development of feelings of political effectiveness as one Latino group. In general, the symbolic benefit of these events demonstrated the efficacy of situational Latino ethnicity by influencing those institutions whose policies affected the collective interests of Puerto Ricans and Mexican Americans.

C. Conference on "Latino Strategies for the '70's"

Another important element of the Spanish Coalition for Jobs that had a bearing upon the emergence and growth of the Latino ethnic group identity and consciousness was its "Latino Strategies for the '70's" conference. This conference was sponsored by the coalition with the aim of promoting the "idea of Latino unity" through a process of communication and dialogue among the participants of the different workshops on issues that concern all Latinos. The overall purpose of the conference was well established in the "Latino Strategies for the '70's—Report" (1973:4):

> [our goal is] to unite ourselves together for better communication, accomplishments and development in political and economic affairs. There should be no barrier on account of our color, language, standard of living. We have to stop thinking we are Mexicans and Puerto Ricans. We have to think of ourselves as Latinos with the belief to feel close together and cooperate with each other; as we suffer together the same needs for lack of representation of Latinos in this country.

The conference's opening statement, as reported in the "Program of Latino Strategies" (1973:3), provides further evidence of the major focus of the event:

> The central purpose of the Strategies for the '70's [conference] is to promote Latino unity. We Latinos have a common language, culture, similar origins and a common purpose; we must come together to work together, for Latino development is both political and economic.
>
> It is essential that we work together. The conference should be viewed as a mechanism for exploring alternative strategies for Latino development. We should define the specific issues to be examined in the workshops. We will have an excellent opportunity to set up priorities among the many areas of need that we will deal with here.

That the "Latino Strategies for the '70's" conference was a direct attempt to promote the Latino ethnic identity can be further inferred from the comments of a Chicano consultant to the conference. In a statement quoted in the conference program (1973:4) he expressed his concerns about the idea of Latino:

> On the eve of the birth of a truly pluralistic society, the Latin American is stirred by the riches of his own diversity. He is not only Latino—though the Latino lies at the core of his being. He is not only American—though Americanhood touches every particle of his life. He is Latin American. This means the intermingling of two histories, many nations, two cultures, two languages, converging, colliding, blending, embracing, depending on one's location within the human geography evolved by one and one-half centuries of relentless interaction.
>
> In words reminiscent of New Testament eschatology, the Latin American is speaking for himself as a new man—a new man for which there is no historical parallel, at least not in the experience of the United States. He speaks of his ethnic family as *LA RAZA*, a new family of man, the first-fruits of a new humanity, where the colors of the Latin American skin, from the darkest to the fairest, will itself be the visible sign of a new age of fraternity. This is the birth of La Nueva Raza. The new breed for a new hope in the Barrio.

The idea of a "Latino conference" was not a new one, for similar efforts had been made a couple of years earlier in Washington, D. C. "The Unidos Conference," as this Washington conference was called, had failed, according to a Spanish Coalition report, because "(1) there was no money to cover costs, (2) there was no staff to work on the conference, and (3) Chicanos and Puerto Ricans were meeting on issues pertaining to their separate communities" (Latino Strategies—Report, 1973:1). The need to avoid similar failures conbined with a feeling that the Spanish Coalition for Jobs "had reached a stage in [its] development where new resources and strategies were needed to maintain and build on the successes of [its] first year" (Proposal to the Rockefeller Foundation, 1972:2). This led the Spanish Coalition for Jobs to seek the assistance of the Chicago Commons Association (one of its well-established organization members), and a proposal was drafted calling for a conference in the spring of 1973.

The proposal was submitted to the Rockefeller Foundation, and six months later a grant of $15,000 was approved. "The original request to the Rockefeller Foundation was for $22,154. [However] $7,400 was provided as in-kind services by member groups" (Proposal to the Rockefeller Foundation, 1972:2).

The Rockefeller Foundation grant enabled the member organization leaders of the Spanish Coalition for Jobs to appoint a conference coordinator during the latter part of 1972. The coordinator began to plan and to develop the conference which had been scheduled for the spring of 1973. As noted in a report issued three months after the conference, "there was a strong-felt need for an area-wide endeavor which would bring all Latinos together in an effort to sort out common problems and consider alternatives for their solution" (Latino Strategies—Report, 1973:1). Or, as indicated in the proposal to the Rockefeller Foundation, "we cannot afford to concentrate all our energies on the single issue of *jobs* while ignoring the many other serious problems confronting our people."

In this way the conference was to provide the forum from which other issues such as housing, education, welfare rights, and the like could be discussed; there was also to be a search for additional structural similarities shared by the several Spanish-speaking ethnics. Much of this search occurred during the conference's many planning sessions, which were held in the Spanish-speaking communities of South Chicago, Pilsen, Lakeview, and Westtown/Humboldt Park. Every evening for nine weeks over 120 persons from different organizations and communities met to discuss strategies and plan the conference. The importance of these sessions was made clear in a progress report submitted to Chicago Commons by the Spanish Coalition for Jobs (October 1972-April 1973: 4): "these sessions brought together, for the first time, Latinos from different organizations and *barrios* to discuss common interests."

Finally, on the weekend of March 16, 1973, the "Latino Strategies for the '70's" conference took place at McCormick Seminary with over 300 persons in attendance. There were 63 representatives of local community organizations in Chicago, 127 staff members of Chicago-based governmental agencies and public and private service organizations, and 41 observers not representing any particular community organization. Forty-six other participants came from outside the Chicago area. As stated in the progress report noted earlier, the community as such was not invited since "it was the purpose of the conference to bring together those individuals who were presently working with agencies and/or organizations [and who were] involved in improving the living conditions of all Latinos" (October 1972–April 1973:4).

During the three days people attended 13 workshops on a wide variety of subjects ranging from employment and housing to health, education, welfare, and others. In all of the sessions the notion of Latinismo was made an explicit part of the presenters' speeches. One of the strongest calls for Latino unity was made by the chair of the employment workshop, who was also one of this study's respondents. According to him, "with Latino we will have Real People's Power [and] with People's Power we will have Political Power."

In a statement presented to the general assembly the first day of the conference the importance of a Latino group identity was reiterated (Latino Strategies for the '70's—Report, 1973:1):

> The brown skin Latino has awakened and he will never be the same again . . . he will never be the same again because he knows that to live is to enjoy freedom. He has learned that to be a Latino is good.
>
> The injustices committed against our people cannot go unchallenged. We must stand by our people. But we can only do it through being united.

In sum, the "Latino Stategies for the '70's" conference was intended to explore alternative strategies for Latino unity and advancement of interests in areas such as education, health and welfare services, housing, and the like. One of the newspapers covering the event viewed it as a successful accomplishment: "The first comprehensive Latino [conference] witnessed the coming together of Latinos from throughout the Midwest to discuss concrete issues for strategy and action" (Newsletter of the Archdiocesan Latin American Committee [N.O.W.], 1973:4).

In the same vein, the coordinator of the education workshop informed me in her interview that the "Latino Strategies" conference resulted in people believing in the idea of Latino. As she put it, "the leadership was buying into the notion of Latinismo. For the first time in Chicago we were talking about working together as one group."

Whether or not the conference accomplished its goals and aims, however, the question remains: Why did the Spanish Coalition for Jobs—an Alinsky-type organization—shift from protest activities where issues were being acted upon to a conference where issues were discussed? One way to think through this shift in issues is to analyze it as an attempt on the part of the Spanish Coalition toward organizational maintenance and growth, as indicated earlier, as well as toward addressing the interests of its member organization leaders.

More specifically, the Spanish Coalition's constituency was made up of the *member organization leaders* and a *mass base of members* from the different organizations. As such, the interests of the two groups of constituents were also somewhat different. For instance, although the Illinois Bell and Jewel issues were pursued for the purpose of organizational maintenance and growth, they were directed, more importantly, toward the attainment of material benefits—jobs—for the coalition's mass base. The issue of the "Latino Strategies for the '70's" conference, on the other hand, corresponded to the interests of the member organizations' leadership in their attempt at organizational maintenance and growth by involving the organizations that were working with issues in areas other than jobs.

As a background for the discussion of interests the following insights on the subject by Pennock (1968:13) are presented:

> When I speak of the interest of a person, or a constituency, or a nation, I mean 'advantage.' An action, policy, law, or institution is in the interest of a person if it increases his opportunity to get what he desires, including the realization of his aspirations and ideals . . . the distinction I am intending to make between 'desire' and 'interest' is the distinction between what is immediately demanded and what in the long run, with the benefit of hindsight, would have been preferred, or would have contributed to the development of the individual into a person capable of making responsible decisions.

In this analysis Pennock fails, however, to make the distinction between subjective and objective interests. An objective (or latent) interest is one which is imputed to members of a group on the basis of shared characteristics; a subjective (or manifest) interest is a conscious and expressed goal of that group. The Spanish Coalition's first two issues, following this line of reasoning, were subjective interests of its *mass-based members*, for they were conscious statements of desirable conditions. The selection and pursuit of the "Latino Strategies" issue involved the transformation of an objective interest into a subjective one. Fish (1973:16) observed a similar process in T.W.O.:

> The selection of issues is a major factor in constituency development. At issue in this context is an interest that has been identified and shaped by a significant 'influence group' and placed within a larger framework of meaning. In short, an issue is a politicized [manifest] interest. . . . Problems are not issues until the interests are lifted up by a group which interprets them in a more comprehensive framework, and furnishes them with tactics that might be pursued to a successful outcome.

Accordingly, organizational maintenance, the preservation of a viable organization by increase in its fundamental base of member organizations, was the stated goal of the *member organization* constituency and was thus a subjective interest. The "Latino Strategies for the '70's" conference represented the selection of an issue meant to satisfy the interest of its member organizations.

My data suggest that prior to the conference the nature of the Spanish Coalition's issue emphasis had contributed to the subjective interests of its mass base. There was concern that the Spanish Coalition's lack of involvement in other issues that concerned citywide Latinos—housing, education, health, and the like—might result in discouragement on the part of some active as well as potential member organization leaders, whose lack of involvement would bring about the demise of the organization.

D. Latino Ethnicity and the Political Activist

The last major sociopolitical development which had a bearing upon the emergence of the Latino ethnicity during this historical period was the conscious role played by one political activist: Hector Franco. The role of Hector Franco appears to have been crucial, since it was he who convinced the other organization leaders that a coalition offered the optimum means of advancing the interests of their respective communities. Thus, Hector Franco brought to the organization's polity a degree of accommodation and association; he provided at least a minimal level of adherence to a set of rules governing the interaction and relationships among the members of the various groups which made up the coalition. These rules constituted a deeply ingrained understanding which transcended the cultural differences dividing the groups, while at the same time binding them at the level of a basic social contract.

It was noted earlier that the Illinois Bell and Jewel job-discrimination issues, as well as the existing social networks of the different community organizations and the Affirmative Action policy, were influential factors that helped to give rise to the development of the Spanish Coalition for Jobs, which became, in turn, the major practitioner and promoter of the Latino group identity in Chicago. Wilson (1973) and others have argued, however, that the mere existence of an issue or a threat and social networks are not sufficient to explain organizational formation: "organizing cadres" are also necessary. According to Wilson (1973:202-3) organizations are more likely to form when

> . . . the need to assert, define, or protest certain precarious values becomes not only an interest of a few would-be leaders, but the pre-occupation of a wider circle of cadres who in turn are able either to mobilize a mass following or to persuade government officials and other audiences to take seriously certain ideas even if they lack a following.

Wilson's discussion builds upon Salisbury's analysis of the role of the "entrepreneur/organizer." To Salisbury (1969:11) the group-formation process involves the selling of the organization by the entrepreneur/organizers to potential members, referred to as investors. That is to say, in order to build a viable organization, the organizers must be able to offer certain benefits to people who agree to become paid-members. When this occurs, "the group is in business," according to Salisbury. Conversely, he argues that "if the benefits fail, or are inadequate to warrant the cost of membership or the leaders get inadequate return, the group collapses" (1969: 11).

Greenstone and Peterson (1973) present another example of the influence of leadership which is suggestive of the importance of other factors as well in the making of an organization. They viewed the leadership of Cesar Chavez as crucial to the success of the farmworkers' movement because it "convinced each individual consumer that his contribution, not eating grapes, would in some small way, increase the probability of supplying the collective. . . . Chavez's leadership thus substituted for the use of comparison or selective inducement to individual contributors" (1972:234). Chavez's effectiveness, then, was a result of his ability to persuade consumers that participation in the grape boycott furthered the achievement of a worthwhile goal, improving the conditions of migrant workers. This suggests that his leadership created what might have been termed "purposive incentives" for organizational involvement noted earlier in the charter: "intangible rewards that derive from the sense of satisfaction of having contributed to the attainment of a worthwhile cause."

Alinsky's (1972) discussion of the building of "People's Organizations" provides further evidence of the practical application of assertions about the values of leadership, social networks, and threats or issues in organizational formation. "Native leadership," according to Alinsky, "was crucial for community organizations" (1972:74). The role of the community organizer (analogous to the organization entrepreneur) involves "identifying these natural leaders and working with them and working for their actual development so that they can become recognized by their following as leaders in more than a limited sphere" (1972:74). The importance of the organizer in performing the critical function of leadership development parallels the central role assigned to entrepreneurs by Salisbury.

In the formation of the Spanish Coalition for Jobs the influence of individuals or organizers/entrepreneurs, rather than cadres, is most indicated. Further, according to my data, it is more accurate to speak of the role played by one leader, Hector Franco, than of the organizers as a group. The impressions which follow are not intended as evidence that the Spanish Coalition for Jobs would not have been formed without this actor; rather, they indicate the function of an individual leader as facilitator of organizational formation.

Hector Franco is a second-generation Puerto Rican who was raised and still resides in the Westtown/Humboldt Park community in the near northwest side of the city. A high-school graduate who had worked for three years in a factory after completing his formal education, Hector Franco began his involvement in community work in 1966, the same year that the Puerto Rican riots occurred in Chicago. His involvement in the field of social service can be seen as almost accidental. As a result of the Puerto Rican riots on Division Street and Damen Avenue in the summer of 1966, the city's power structure was alerted to the presence of yet another disadvantaged Spanish-speaking minority group. The Department of Human Resources opened an outpost (the first in any of the city's Spanish-speaking *barrios*) to defuse the political activities of the Puerto Rican community. As expressed by Hector Franco:

> I went to Puerto Rico in 1966 for a vacation, and I was there when the riots started. It was also in Puerto Rico that I began to read about police brutality and the way Puerto Ricans in Chicago were being abused by the police. So right after the riots the Chicago Community Renewal Opportunity [an offshoot of the Department of Human Resources] began to solicit people to do 'community rep work': work in the community. Although I knew very little about community work, I applied for the job and got it.

Eventually Hector Franco and eleven others who were hired to work for this human resources outpost went on to become the initial members of the first Urban Progress Center staffed by Spanish-speaking in Chicago. It was during the three and one-half years that he worked for the Urban Progress Center that Hector Franco learned about community work and organizing activities. He worked as a supervisor, interviewer, and program coordinator. Hector Franco became frustrated with the "system's way of doing things" when the small store-front agency with its limited space, resources, and personnel proposed to provide an array of services to the Puerto Rican community. He was certain that "in reality, this outpost was meant to pacify and quiet down the situation in Westtown."

In fact it was a black resident of Westtown, Sally Johnson, who convinced Hector Franco that "community organizing" was the proper direction for the poor rather than the direct service approach utilized by community agencies. The two met in 1968, when Sally Johnson joined the staff of the Division Street Urban Progress Center. Sally Johnson became one of Hector Franco's closest associates, a fact reflected in his discussion of her:

> When Sally came in, I trained her and worked with her in terms of recruiting additional community representatives. Sally lived on Bell Street near Division. She was very active and she started to move and reach out for the need to work together as Puerto Ricans and blacks. At the time she also started to deal with the Urban Training Center on Christian Mission. This center was basically one that dealt with community organizing. So imagine—she was working for the city and at the same time she was working in organizing. That was really inspiring. When she got caught doing community organizing while being on the city's payroll, she decided to leave the city job. It was not very difficult for me to leave with her.

In 1969 Hector Franco and Sally Johnson quit their jobs with the Division Street Urban Progress Center to enter into the field of community organizing. They formed the Allies for a Better Community (A.B.C.) organization. A.B.C. was formed primarily as a response to the displacement of Puerto Rican and black residents from the Division and Bell Street area. As Hector Franco informed me in my second interview with him, "we left the Urban Progress Center and immediately we started to organize people around the issue of Urban Renewal and Saint Mary's [a hospital located in Westtown] attempt to move us from that area in order to build a new hospital."

Although the "fight against Saint Mary's" turned out to be an unsuccessful one, the significance of this earlier involvement in community organizing lies in the support that A.B.C. received from the Coalition for United Community Action—a black organization in which Sally Johnson participated. Conversely, A.B.C. eventually joined the Coalition for United Community Action, becoming the only

Spanish-speaking organization in the coalition. In 1969 this coalition had begun to pressure the Chicago and Cook County Building Trades Council to hire minorities in the construction industry. Subsequently this pressure resulted in the signing of an agreement between the two organizations in January 1970 to incorporate minorities in this field.

That A.B.C.'s participation in the Coalition for United Community Action was of vital importance for Hector Franco's development and growth as an organizer can be inferred from his description of the coalition's effect on A.B.C.:

> I received some good organizing training by participating in the Coalition for United Community Action. One of the things that they did was to develop a Black Strategy Center that provided resources and training in community organizing. I picked up on the Alinsky model of organizing and much more. Organizing 100 people in order to get the city to put up a stop sign was not enough. That is important but Latinos in the city of Chicago have greater needs, such as housing, jobs, education, and so on. So basically, I wanted to build a coalition of Latino organizations to deal with an issue that was affecting all of us equally.

A year after joining the Coalition for United Community Action Hector Franco withdrew A.B.C. as a member organization of the coalition because of rumors and allegations that the coalition's executive director had embezzled money from its funding grant. For the next year Hector Franco's efforts went into building A.B.C. as a "powerful community organization." In addition to this task he was also concerned with the idea of building a "coalition of Latino organizations."

Hector Franco's vision of a "citywide Latino coalition" apparently had become easier to realize, since during this time Puerto Rican and Mexican American workers were being excluded from the labor force of major American corporations. Accordingly, the situation appeared to be conducive for the creation or construction of a "Latino organization" or coalition. As Hector Franco stated:

> Let me say that at that time it was not so difficult to get people to buy into the Latino idea because it was self-interest. The self-interest was that different employment agencies, such as Association House, Una Puerto Abierta, and others from Pilsen as well as from Westtown, were facing an up-the-hill struggle with corporations in terms of getting jobs for Latinos. So as a result of that problem, or that common need (which was the thing that we had in common), we were able to work out our differences. And people knew that this coalition was representing their interests or that it would be to their advantage to join. We even had Ochoa's group from the Cardinal's Committee from 18th Street. At that time people were focusing on coming together for the purpose of giving strength to a group or groups that ordinarily were powerless or had been powerless. So that we knew that in the Westtown area, doing the Puerto Rican thing alone was not going to solve the problem. I also think that the Chicano community held the same position. Thus in some issues we could deal as Puerto Ricans and in others, particularly those that had city-wide impact, we need to move as Latinos. Even to this day we still have that phenomenon taking place.

Correspondingly, Hector Franco's task as the "entrepreneur or leader" of a Latino coalition was not only to create the belief that everyone's participation was necessary for the accomplishment of the organization's aims but also to foster the impression that by participating, individuals could influence the nature of these objectives. He offered two incentives to the leaders of the member organizations: a sense of accomplishment from working together and the opportunity to place individual Puerto Rican and Mexican and Mexican American interests among the organization's priorities. In the view of Alinsky (1972:119) the organizer, in order to induce the participation of potential members of community organizations, must show "that [an] organization will give them power, the ability, the strength, the force to be able to do something" about the problems. This activity is a form of "manipulation of expectations" which Frohlich et al. (1971) have considered as central to the role of the organizational entrepreneur; it can also be characterized as the development of feelings of political efficacy.

In sum, in the Spanish Coalition for Jobs Hector Franco and his associates (the cochairs of the organization), as well as different leaders who helped form the coalition, made the first organizing effort which gave meaning to the idea of Latinismo in Chicago. The Spanish Coalition for Jobs was clearly seen as an attempt to do "something Latino" through the tactics of protests and confrontations. As one of the coalition's members from that period expressed in his second interview:

> The Spanish Coalition for Jobs is very responsible for giving significance to Latinismo in Chicago. The Latino concept became a reality, something concrete and real. People knew that Latinos were those folks out on the streets doing things for themselves. Another significant impact was that it was able to put together a coalition composed of Latinos across the city. This was often considered an impossibility by a lot of people.

Conversely, when the organization shifted its emphasis from a protest organization to direct service, its identity as a "Latino community organization" seemed to have disappeared as well. After pressuring Illinois Bell and Jewel Tea to agree to contracts or concessions to employ Latinos and after its celebrated "Latino Strategies for the '70's" conference discussed earlier, the Spanish Coalition for Jobs went on to become another community organization providing direct services to the residents of the Pilsen community. As a result, the efforts of the coalition were transferred from citywide Latino concerns to community-oriented ones, servicing primarily the Mexican American residents of that area. Hector Franco offers one account which describes what happened to the Spanish Coalition for Jobs:

> The Spanish Coalition for Jobs, as direct action and active group, went into another direction. It went into social service provider in the area of employment. We had a confrontation and there was a split between the leadership of Westtown and

> that of Pilsen. At that time, the regional director of SER [Educational Vocational Development and Employment Opportunities] for Jobs came in saying that we had outgrown the time; that direct action in the form of picketing and boycotts was out and that times called for more sophistication. [My concern was, however, that] if it became a direct service provider, which community was going to receive the services? If the Spanish Coalition, as such, was going to be based in Pilsen, how were the Puerto Ricans going to benefit from its services? And if we had it here in Westtown, I'm sure that the Mexican leadership was going to scream.

Another explanation about the transition of the Spanish Coalition for Jobs is offered by the director of the organization:

> The Spanish Coalition for Jobs has changed mostly in its scope. I felt that we could holler and scream as much as we wanted out in the streets, but if we did not start delivering services and implementing some kind of meaningful program to maintain our credibility, then nothing was going to happen. It was at this time that Operation SER for Jobs came into the picture. The people from Westtown did not want them because they were out of town: not Puerto Rican enough or too Mexican. Basically, Operation SER, which had the national visibility, wanted to name the coalition to reflect their name. Immediately flashes went up and people started to envision takeover politics. We stayed together and in late 1974 started negotiating our first contract with the Mayor's Office for Manpower.

With the co-optation of protest, the Spanish Coalition for Jobs entered into what may be termed its second phase, as a direct service organization. Along with this shift Hector Franco's role as one of the leading advocates of the idea of Latino in Chicago was also reduced. Needless to say, his contribution toward the construction or adaptation of the idea of Latino ethnicity as a mobilizing political force can be measured in the successes of the Spanish Coalition for Jobs.

CONCLUSION

In this chapter we have examined the major events that created the situations used for the adoption and application of the idea of a Latino group identity by Puerto Rican and Mexican American leaders in Chicago during the early years of the 1970s decade. The issue of job discrimination by Illinois Bell and Jewel, as well as the significant role played by the Affirmative Action legal policy, served as the leading developments in the emergence of this type of group form through the organizational efforts of the Spanish Coalition for Jobs. The Spanish Coalition's identity as a Latino organization reinforces the idea that Latino ethnicity has significance in certain situational contexts; it is constructed around issues common to both Puerto Ricans and Mexican Americans.

The Spanish Coalition's victories showed to its Mexican American and Puerto Rican mass-based constituency that they could get such material benefits, as jobs, by working together as one Latino group. In other words, the coalescing of the different organizations' mass base to form the Spanish Coalition's membership begins to give weight to the notion that Puerto Ricans and Mexican Americans shared not only language commonality but structural similarities as well. Further, these were activated in the form of Latino ethnic mobilization by the legitimate claim provided by the Affirmative Action policy. Thus the coincidence of internal and external factors play significantly in the formation of Latino ethnic mobilization.

As far as structural conditions that give rise to and maintain Latino ethnic affinity, and the circumstances which may spark Latino ethnic mobilization, I agree with Ragin (1972: 622) that "there is a parallel to those structural conditions described by Marx (1852) and Engels (1848) as conducive to class solidarity. These include substantial economic inequality, the perception of this inequality as part of a pattern of collective oppression, and adequate communication among members of the oppressed." In other words, at the center of Latino ethnic affinity and mobilization are the structural and circumstantial conditions of working-class solidarity and action. Conversely, what I am introducing here is an organizational transactional approach in which the traditional ethnic cultural markers are changed or substituted with membership flow across boundaries from various ethnic groups to form a larger numerical ethnic entity. Consequently, the creation of a Latino ethnic unit is based on the interdependency of a cultural element (language) on broader social structural conditions not in themselves ethnic at all.

In sum, the chapter points to the socioeconomic and political power distributions in Chicago which result in Puerto Ricans and Mexican Americans experiencing the very same structured inequalities. These power distributions generated political entrepreneurs with consciousness and interest in mobilizing these groups as one Latino unit for the purpose of altering such systems of structured inequality. In other words, persistent patterns of structured inequality have created systematic uniformities in the environments of Puerto Ricans and Mexican Americans in Chicago which produce, in turn, similarities of experiences, basic orientations, and patterns of behavior. Thus, Latino ethnic consciousness may be seen partly as a response to the more general perception of the intensification of these systematic conditions.

Further, it is also important to recognize that the activation of Latino ethnic mobilization was made possible by the Affirmative Action policy. The policy legitimated the collective claims made by Mexican American and Puerto Rican leaders. Thus, it needs to be seen that the shifting of flexible boundaries may also originate from forces outside the groups. For Latino ethnic mobilization is the result of the coincidence of internal and external forces.

4

The Legitimation of Latino Identity:

The Case of the Latino Institute

The preceeding chapter showed that Latino ethnic group identity and behavior represent a wider group identification for at least two Spanish-speaking groups (Mexican Americans and Puerto Ricans), interacting during certain situational contexts to gain advantages or overcome disadvantages in American society. It was shown how this type of group identity was created and expressed by the Spanish Coalition for Jobs and how this organization was subsequently transformed into a Mexican American service agency, reducing the idea of a Latino ethnic identity to the status of a "loosely used label" which lacked its collectively politicized and mobilizing significance. In other words, with the transformation of the Spanish Coalition for Jobs into an organization with rigidly defined Mexican American ethnic boundaries, there was no longer a group to effectively embody the goals of the "Latino movement" in the city.

Before a significant Latino social movement could develop among the various Spanish-speaking groups, there had to be created a new structure to bring "Latino" sympathizers together. To be sure, the creation of a new organization, the Latino Institute, came to represent the main source of adherents for such movement and activities. For the founders of the Latino Institute there was indeed a single Latino community identification that only needed to be reorganized or reshaped. Nagel and Olzak (1982:129) refer to this process as resurgence: "a renascence of ethnic sentiment and organization among a formerly mobilized, though recently inactive, ethnic group." The new organization, then, would work to reunite this community and become the force behind Latino mobilization in Chicago.

CHICAGO COMMONS

The development of the Latino Institute was heavily influenced by the work of the Chicago Commons Association, a type of settlement house located in the Westtown/Humboldt Park community. The Chicago Commons Association was originally established in 1894 in the Near West Side, several miles south from its present-day location. During the 1950s urban renewal projects forced the relocation of the organization; this change required that services provided by Chicago Commons be modified to meet the needs of Puerto Rican newcomers to this particular neighborhood. Perhaps because its participation as a member organization of the Spanish Coalition for Jobs, or its earlier involvement with Mexican Americans in the Near West Side (among the various groups that the organization worked with), the major aim of Chicago Commons was to help establish a "Latino base of power" in Chicago. It can be said that during this time Chicago Commons represented the major network most "cooptable" to the idea of a Latino movement in this Midwest metropolis. "To be cooptable, [an organization] must be composed of like-minded people whose backgrounds, experiences, or location in the social structure make them receptive to the ideas of a specific new movement" according to Freeman (1983:9). Like other social-movement organizations, the Latino Institute required some outside assistance in the form of funds or personnel to serve as a catalyst for the Latino movement process. Forms of social control, insufficient information, and lack of experience in movement activities necessitated certain resources unavailable to the city's Spanish-speaking residents. Chicago Commons, thus, came to represent for the Latino Institute the ongoing infusion of outside resources which made the latter's program feasible. These resources included knowledge of the problem, access to professional expertise, and expressions of legitimacy from outside authorities.

The decision of the Chicago Commons Association to promote and help give rise to a Latino ethnic solidarity coincided with the ambitions of Hector Franco, the former chair of the Spanish Coalition for Jobs, to establish a "Latino institute." The organization, according to Hector Franco, was to represent a communication network for Spanish-speaking residents in the city. Several of my respondents identified Hector Franco as the person most responsible for developing the idea of an institute. In the words of one participant in the "Latino Strategies for the '70's" conference:

> . . . I do know that if there is one single individual who you could argue is responsible for that event [the Latino Strategies conference], it would be Hector Franco. The Latino Institute was a stem of the conference because that was in effect the outcome of the Latino Strategies: to institutionalize it.

To Hector Franco the Latino Institute was not necessarily the sole or direct result of the conference on Latino strategies. Instead he sees the institute's beginning in the following way:

> Some people claim that the Latino Institute was born out of the conference. However, it goes back to the days when A.B.C. was involved with the black coalition. The black coalition formed a strategies center to bring together black professionals and resources and to provide the technical assistance which would contribute to the black struggle. This idea of a strategies center stayed in my mind and I had this thing that we needed something like that for the Spanish-speaking. I talked to the Associate Director of Chicago Commons, who was black, and

> we initiated talks with other people in Commons. Eventually the idea ended up with the person in charge of program development and he wrote the proposal for it.

In an interview the director of Chicago Commons indicated that his organization began to work with Hector Franco to develop the idea of an institute because "he represented the only organization with a designed program for the community." The director added, "We were even talking about the idea of an institute back then [in 1969]." When I asked the director of commons to explain what he meant, he said:

> When I first became the director of commons in 1968, on several occasions different groups of Puerto Rican community organization leaders met with me to make me aware of the needs and problems of the community. They figured that since I was new, I did not know what was going on. They would come to my office, and we would talk for a while, but they would never come back with a solid proposal. Well, Hector [Franco] was the only one that visited me more than one time. And he had some solid ideas that we felt we could work with. One of those ideas was a Latino Institute—a center to bring the different Latino organizations together.

From these early discussions plans emerged to seek funds to design and implement a Latino Institute. Before this could be done, the Chicago Commons Association requested that evidence be given to justify the need for such an entity. Correspondingly, a conference ("Latino Strategies for the '70's" discussed earlier) was planned to identify and discuss the most pressing areas of concern in the city's Puerto Rican and Mexican American communities. The conference's various panel discussions were used in part to generate needs-assessment and recommendations, including that for establishing an institute. These were in turn to be used in the search for necessary funding.

The process of following up on the conference's suggestion to found an institute moved very slowly, not reaching culmination until a year later. Most of the intervening time was used designing and preparing a suitable organizational structure. In the spring of 1974 the proceedings of the conference were finally used by Chicago Commons to write a grant proposal seeking funds for the development and implementation of the recommended organization. This proposal was submitted to the Community Fund of Chicago in March 1974. Chicago Commons' proposal was primarily meant to secure "seed money," that is, a short-term two-year grant, to develop a center which would service "Latinos" citywide. It was anticipated that within two years the new organization would be an entity on its own and capable of expanding on the original grant.

Several months after the submission of this proposal Chicago Commons received a two-year grant of $70,000 from the Community Fund of Chicago ("Latino Institute Proposal to the Lilly Endowment, Inc.," Sept. 16, 1975:3). In this way Chicago Commons became the fiscal agent of the new organization. Three staff members were hired, including the institute's executive director, Maria Cerda, a Puerto Rican.

For the first three months of its existence the Latino Institute conducted its functions out of the offices of the Chicago Commons Association in the Puerto Rican community of Westtown. In January 1975 the new organization moved downtown to 105 S. LaSalle Street. The location of the organization was of great significance for the institutionalization and legitimation of the "Latino group identity." Basically this meant centralizing the location of the organization to prevent or avoid being identified with one specific group. I was informed of the importance of this central location by several former staff members of the Latino Institute. One declared: "We would not have been a Latino Institute over in Pilsen because we would have faced the problem of favoring Mexicans. How can we profess to be a Latino Institute in Pilsen or Westtown?"

Maria Cerda offers another account of the importance of having the Latino Institute centrally located downtown:

> . . . the Task Force [board members], as well as I, felt that if we were going to look into leadership development or something that would have an impact on the whole Latino community, we could not put an organizer working on issues on every corner. And in order to do that I could not be in a storefront on Division Street or in Pilsen. Our efforts could only come out of downtown because we wanted not only to tap the [communities'] internal leadership but also the leadership of the city: the power-makers and policy-makers. We wanted to establish a presence as Latinos united, and for that we needed to be where the power is wielded, which is downtown.

As noted, in its initial stages the Latino Institute functioned with a staff of three. This staff served several important functions. First, recruitment of a large membership of supporters of the concept of a "Latino Institute" was seen as essential to the organization's goal of becoming the voice of the city's "Latino community." That is to say, if the Latino Institute was to serve as the mechanism to sustain a cohesion of Latino group identity and consciousness, the organization needed to build a strong base of support for the organization's philosophy. According to Maria Cerda membership recruitment became her initial and primary task as executive director of the organization:

> I spent most of my time contacting, visiting, and informing the directors of the different agencies that this was what I had in mind, and what did they think about it. I visited people in Pilsen, Westtown, and everywhere. We mainly met with the many organizations to inform them that this was what we were doing and that we did not know where we were going but that we have some ideas. Many agreed with my directions and many others did not.

Another important task of the Latino Institute's limited staff was that of securing its own funding base. In other words, if one of the goals was to become an autonomous entity representing the collective needs and interests of the Spanish-speaking, the new organization could not function very long as an "arm" of the Chicago Commons Association. As a result, the organization wrote its first proposal, calling for five program components with the major emphasis placed on "leadership development." One of the organization's original staff members informed me that the leadership component was given priority because of "the continuous discussion during the Latino strategies conference about the need to develop sophisticated leadership with the capacity to function and express itself well and effectively."

In any event, the organization wrote its initial proposal and six months later was awarded a three-year grant of $400,000 by the Rockefeller Foundation. Basically the grant funded the organization's major component in the form of "leadership development of parents in bilingual education." One of the Latino Institute's former staff members defined the leadership component in the following way:

> . . . to provide parents with good updated information about bilingual education, what bilingual education was, models for bilingual education classes, their rights and privileges and similar things. It was also meant to facilitate skill development in planning, in evaluation, in how to run a meeting, how to relate to one another and to the outside world. To become better advocates for bilingual education. And to change the attitude that they had about themselves and about not wanting to get involved because they did not speak English.

Although not necessarily the type of leadership program that the organization had defined originally, the implementation of the new parent leadership component did lead to the expansion of the organization's staff. From the original three the Latino Institute grew with the addition of five trainers and two assistant technical resource persons. Further, by securing its initial grant the Latino Institute achieved the goal of becoming an autonomous entity long before the initial program expansion grant from the Chicago Community Fund had expired. It received its 501-C3 (tax-exempt status) as well as its first major operating grant from a major funding source.

In the main the establishment of the Latino Institute in 1974 was viewed as the creation of a highly systematic and orchestrated effort meant to eliminate the obstacles which had frustrated the attempts of the Spanish-speaking in improving the quality of their life in the city ("Latino Institute: History and Philosophy," mimeographed). The Latino Institute was formed to seek economic and social progress, self-determination, and to impact those institutions and agencies that stood in the way of the progress of the various Spanish-speaking communities. To members of both the Latino Institute and Chicago Commons this was to be accomplished by the "legitimation" of Latinismo or Hispanismo. This meant that the Latino Institute strove for recognition by the city power structure of the collective Spanish-Speaking groups' viability in the polity of the larger society. The members of the new organization realized that, in words of Kilson (1975:239), "the power-mustering dimension of ethnicity appears to endow it with legitimacy in American life." This process of ethnic legitimation corresponds to the idea of the politicization of ethnicity discussed earlier. A variety of groups in American society legitimized or politicized their ethnicity by integrating into the expanding industrial urban economy or by using the political arena of some of the major cities in the nation. For the founders of the Latino Institute Chicago's Spanish-speaking represented one of the latest social groups which would utilize this approach. The members of the organization also proclaimed that "Latino or Hispanic legitimation" in Chicago was incomplete. Hence their attempt to realize the power-creating capability of a Latino community or population.

The Latino Institute, in turn, attempted to legitimize Latinismo by "bargaining" with the target group—the group whose behavior the organization was trying to influence. (In this case the city's power structure represented the target of the new organization.) According to Turner (1970:148) "bargaining takes place when the movement has control over some exchangeable value that the target group wants and offers some of that value in return for compliance with its demands." How does a social movement, which lacks the legitimacy of existing institutions and whose purpose is to challenge tradition, establish a claim to authority? According to the founders of the institute this was the problem confronted by the Spanish-speaking community in Chicago, for to be successful—to create political resources by gaining sympathetic public attention—the Latino movement needed to establish credibility with various outsiders. From this point of view the role of the Latino Institute was to be that of devising techniques for establishing credibility and legitimacy with those who might otherwise be indifferent or hostile to the Spanish-speaking community.

The new organization offered to deliver the support of an "ever-growing" Latino community destined to be of significant importance to the political and economic life of society. That there was no longer a need to fear Latino radicalism as long as the institute was the mouthpiece of the populations was the general claim made by the founders and members of the organization. The essence of coercion (e.g., the threat of harm) was perceived by members of the institute as being more costly in arousing suspicion and resistance in the long run; the "traditional integrationist" program of the organization eschewed protest or coercion as unacceptable and/or ineffective. Overall it was assumed that the more tough-minded and pragmatic business and governmental leaders would be more responsive to the bargaining appeals and approaches of the Latino Institute.

CONTROVERSY OVER THE INSTITUTE

The decision to utilize a bargaining strategy, as opposed to the coercive method employed by the Spanish Coalition for Jobs against its targeted groups, had a major consequence for the new organization. The problem revolved around the type of Latino identification needed to be expressed and/or presented by the Latino Institute in its efforts to legitimize Latinismo. One group argued that the most appropriate Latino identity for the new organization to adopt would be that which emanated from the more high-status and educated Spanish-speaking professionals. This idea was based on the premise that to be affective, the expression of Latino identity and behavior by members of the organization required approximating closely the social-class culture and aspirations of the people that the new organization was most likely to interact with from its downtown location. The other group, represented primarily by Hector Franco, argued that the new entity needed to integrate the perspective of local-level community organizations into its structure. In this way the so-called *barrio* (neighborhood) politics could become an important dimension of the institute's identity and ideological base.

What appears to have occurred is that following the "Latino Strategies for the '70's" conference, part of the grass-roots-level leadership, which organized the event, was chosen to serve on a "steering committee," or task force. This committee was organized by Chicago Commons to design the most adequate organizational structure or plan for the new organization. The local-level *barrio* leaders, however, were excluded from participating in the committee's important policy-making activities which eventually gave definition and structure to the organization. As Hector Franco remarked in my second interview with him:

> The proposal which was submitted to the Rockefeller people had set up a board structure that had Chicago Commons as the board of directors with their *gringos* [whites] and those Latinos that were recommended by us. My biggest mistake was to recommend to this board people like . . . . . . who were upper class in their views. My initial thing with. . . . .— the first chairman of the board of directors of the Institute—

was that we felt that there should have been more people that were involved in the conference partaking in this thing [the Latino Institute]. The grass-roots organizations responsible for giving rise to the Latino Institute should serve on the board of the organization as well as forming part of its staff.

In the same interview I asked Hector Franco to explain why the "*barrio* people" had been left out of the new organization. He responded:

> Possibly because we used unorthodox methods. Those methods clashed with those of the Institute. For instance, if we had been involved, I don't think that the Institute would be located downtown today. Also, the whole concept of a Latino Institute was changed from the original idea. Initially the Latino Institute was supposed to be a technical resource arm of the Latino community. By that I mean that if you have X, Y, and Z organizations and they need about $30,000 to function, the Institute's job was to work with this organization to help it get the $30,000. In addition to that, my idea was that if I get $300,00 in grants, I would distribute that equally to groups that needed the funding. But the people on the board and those heading the institute did not believe in that or in advocacy. They did not believe in direct action. Any issue that was controversial would be thrown into the community. I think that once we stop protesting, progress will stop.

In the same vein, although not favoring Hector Franco's suggestion of a "philanthropic role" for the Latino Institute, one of the study's respondents recalls that during the conference on Latino strategies there were some talks about a "central place that would receive funds to be distributed to other agencies." The same respondent further explains this idea in the following way:

> Originally the Latino Institute was supposed to play some kind of a role like that, but the problem was that the Latino Institute becomes a structure by itself and in fact competed with other groups for funds or grants. It was easier to give $1,000 to the Latino Institute in the name of the Latino community than to

> have to give something to A.B.C., Casa Aztlan, Uptown, and other organizations.

The board members of the Chicago Commons Association and the founders of the Latino Institute worried, with some basis in reality, that some Spanish-speaking among them might introduce into "middle-class America" the more radical conceptions of *barrio* struggle which had comprised the programs of the Spanish Coalition for Jobs. A *barrio*-type of Latino identification and behavior would have functioned in opposition to the expectations of mainstream middle-class America. This view is understandable since the leaders and founders of the Latino Institute were middle-class reformers, more prominent and less alienated from mainstream America than the members of the Spanish Coalition for Jobs. In this respect the Latino Institute was more elitist in character than the local-level organizations such as the Spanish Coalition for Jobs.

The acceptance of mainstream middle-class culture, on the other hand, seemed to have resulted in what may be perceived as the understatement or suppression of the Latino-conscious behavior expressed by *barrio* residents. This point is well illustrated in a rather long quote by one of the study's respondents, who also served as one of the presidents of the Board of Directors of the Latino Institute:

> Hector [Franco] didn't want anything to do with the Latino Institute eventually. One of the great problems that we have is that any Latino organization that wants to be connected to the funding sources of the establishment needs to achieve respectable status. This is usually done by the criteria set up by the establishment. The constant problems that you have are how to meet the needs of the lower class through a structure that has middle-class respectability. That is the damn problem. And if you want to regulate the poor, then you need to reach them in the front line exactly where the poor are coming from. In so doing, you have to hire people who are representatives of the poor, and in so doing, you're running an organization that never meets the criteria of the middle class and the respect-

> ability of the system. It's a contradiction. On the other hand, you have to have someone with a public image like Maria Cerda who was a member of the Board of Education; whose husband is a judge; who can meet with the mayor; who could meet with people from Marshall Field's. You need a board of respectable sponsors. You need to work with people from the First National Bank. In order to do that, you have to be like them. We decided to establish an agency that promoted the latter. The real problem was that people like Hector Franco did not have the credibility and respectability of the system because of who he is. He lives a life-style that is really *barrio* life-style. He mingles, talks, and lives, and he is an extension of that.

And, in a different way, the answer given by Chicago Commons' director to the question of why a particular person was chosen for the job of director of the Latino Institute serves as further evidence of the perceived suppression of Latino identity as expressed by *barrio* residents:

> She was more cosmopolitan. She could deal in the corporate world. She had just finished her tenure as a Board of Education member. She had excellent contacts and was well known and liked by Latinos citywide. It seems to me that she was perfect or just made for that position.

The interethnic controversy, which highlighted the formation of the Latino Institute (and which many people believe to exist today), can be interpreted by looking at how Chicago Commons influenced the particular expression of Latino identity and behavior adopted by the organization. Whether the Latino Institute has been able to attain the authenticity and recognition for the "Latino ethnic group" in Chicago is beyond the scope of this study. What is clear is that the Latino Institute's definition of a Latino frame was significantly determined or shaped by the expectations of the Chicago Commons Association. Given the weak ties between the new organization and other Puerto Rican and Mexican American organizations, the greater was the tendency to rely upon support from the Chicago Commons Association, and thus to have strategies limited by the conditions imposed from outside. Chicago Commons, in other words, determined the Latino Institute's conscious policies as well as serving as foci for the latter's values and activities.

The founding members of the Latino Institute were also aware that "outsiders" held stereotypes of "Latinos" (as they do of every minority group), and the members knew the content of these stereotypes; as a result, they came to oppose this stereotypic image and behavior. Or as Lyman and Douglass (1973:347) would contend: "These members see themselves as inheritors of a symbolic ethnic estate whose saliencies and rank order or priorities are sharply and sometimes inversely differentiated from the perspective of the larger group." From this point of view it is safe to suggest that the founding members of the Latino Institute attempted some form of "collective impression management" as they sought to defuse potentially dangerous aspects of the stereotypic saliencies or manifestation of Latino identity and behavior operative in the city's various Spanish-speaking *barrios*.

Conversely, the perception of the larger social system held by the founders of the Latino Institute was based on the predisposition that the larger American society could be responsive or even manipulative if Latino identification and behavior corresponded with that of middle-class, mainstream America. Thus, the organization was designed to bring into the society those elements which the latter recognized as legitimate, while withholding from presentation any element which challenged the "subverted cherished values" of the American society. Dahl (1961:35-36) explains this practice by saying, "When members of ethnic minorities have depended for greater opportunities on the acceptance of the dominant group, they have found it desirable to decrease impact of the ethnic stigma." It was assumed that such a stigma was embodied in the ideology and behavior of *barrio* residents; local-level community organizations were also viewed as the transmitters of this stigmatized image. While not denying ethnic allegiances to the *barrio* groups and residents, the founders of the Latino Institute pursued particular efforts to make *barrio*-based politics and expressions of Latino ethnic identity and behavior less burdensome by improving the image of the group.

There are many cases of interethnic controversy similar to the one experienced by the Latino Institute. One such example is offered by Banfield and Wilson (1963). Using a "socioeconomic stratification model" to explain this kind of group segmentation, Banfield and Wilson show that when such groups are called upon to vote for a political candidate of their own ethnic group, for instance, it is better to have one who does not seem to cater too exclusively to members in the lower strata and who does not seem to conform to the ethnic stereotype held by the dominant group, but who can give "desirable recognition" to the group in the wider society (1963:43).

An earlier and more specific case of interethnic controversy or conflict is offered by Frazier in a study on the historical decline of skin-color status groups among blacks in the United States in the 1930s (rev. 1966). Also through an explanation in socioeconomic terms Frazier suggests that the chasm between the lighter-skinned upper strata of the black community and the lower-class newcomers has been the most widely known expression of the problem of ethnic solidarity in the black community as the stream of migrants has continued to flow with greater or lesser force since emancipation (1966:295). The former have reacted, Frazier argues, as have the more advantaged in other groups, by trying to maintain the social distance as well as by extending some assistance to the less fortunate through philanthropic and uplift organizations. He concludes, however, that discord seems to have been strong during most periods, and since such a great proportion of the black group is even now in the very lowest stratum of the society, discord is noticeable among segments which are not far apart in socioeconomic terms.

One major inference that can be drawn from this is that

barrio politics and its definition of "social reality" are not necessarily the only features of movement organizations like the Latino Institute. This is a particular case of a movement organization which emerged, grew, and survived out of more than just feelings of frustration or deprivation on the part of an aggrieved population. The case of the Latino Institute corresponds to the McCarthy and Zald (1973) definition of modern social movements. They see the rise of professional movement organizations made up primarily of personnel committed to social movement careers as more important than individual citizen participation to the vitality of a social movement.

In fact, to the Latino Institute the Latino ethnic identity expressed by *barrio* groups and residents seemed a liability to the organization's survival; hence, the institute found it pointless or even counterproductive to activate such an identification and consciousness. For this reason the organization decided to adopt a low profile or, indeed, even leave the "political arena" for a period of time. This is not tantamount to depoliticizing or demolishing the group. Rothschild (1982:8) comments that a group decision to withdraw from the more politicized arena as a "corporate combatant" can be seen as a sophisticated political strategy in the interest of group survival and legitimation. In any event, the case of the Latino Institute illustrates that the concept of Latino or Hispanic has a variegated and flexible repertoire of political options: Latino ethnic identity and mobilization in the form of *barrio* ideological sentiments or as a middle-class form of identification and behavior. In both instances the construction and expression of Latino ethnic identity is based on the most useful and strategic way of using a large-scale Latino unit as a mobilizing force in the polity of the city of Chicago. And in both cases the actors make use of Latinismo as a maneuver or strategem in working out their chances within the system of inequality of the larger American society. Further, although their tactics differed markedly, the Latino Institute and local-level groups like the Spanish

Coalition for Jobs had an identical goal—full participation in an integrated society. Each organization carved out a unique program, style, and mode of operation that broadened the Latino movement's support base by offering a range of organizational alternatives from which potential members and benefactors could choose.

Both cases of the Latino Institute and Spanish Coalition for Jobs serve as further evidence that the Latino ethnic unit (for that matter, ethnicity in general) is a socially constructed and used feature of human identity, available for employment by participants in an encounter and subject to presentation, inhibition, manipulation, and exploitation. The manipulation of Latino ethnic identity and saliencies, however, is not totally unrestricted. Barth (1969:25), for instance, recognizes both the potential for identity ploys and their limitations when he states:

> Different circumstances obviously favor different performances. Since ethnic identity is associated with a culturally specific set of value standards, it follows that there are circumstances where such an identity can be moderately successfully realized, and limits beyond which such success is precluded. I will agree that ethnic identities will not be retained beyond these limits, because allegiances to basic value standards will not be sustained where one's own comparative performance is utterly inadequate. The two components in this relative measure of success are, first, the performance of others and, second, the alternatives open to oneself. . . . What matters is how well the others, with whom one interacts and to whom one is compared, manage to perform, and what alternative identities and sets of standards are available to the individual.

From this point of view, certain contrasting factors or influences played significant roles in shaping the way that both the Spanish Coalition for Jobs and the Latino Institute developed and expressed their distinct versions of Latino ethnic identification. Further, as each organization was fully cognizant of its particular geographical location—its environment or turf—this required adapting appropriate "behavioral patterns" as Latinos. The Latino Institute chose to make inroads in middle-class America; its central location was among downtown corporations and finance centers, as one of my study participants indicated above. To criticize the kind of Latino identification formulated and expressed by the Latino Institute as being middle class or elitist or that of the Spanish-Coalition for Jobs as barrio-style is, I feel, unsound without examining and analyzing those factors that shape the various expressions of this wider-scale identification. I argue instead that the construction of the Latino ethnic identity is rarely ever the sole function of one isolated party or group. In this process of identity formation and negotiation, awareness of how the wider society weighs and ranks group behavior plays a significant part. For the Latino Institute, knowledge of the ideology or stereotype of the wider society toward minority-group conduct was a leading factor in the selection of the expression of Latino-related behavior.

The activities of the Spanish Coalition for Jobs laid the groundwork for the future movement in two significant ways: (1) it unearthed ample evidence of the unequal status of the Spanish-speaking and in the process convinced many previously uninterested Spanish-speakers that something should be done; (2) it created a climate of expectations that something would be done. The development of the Latino Institute added to the Latino movement a quite distinct network. As a result, the movement has two origins, from two different strata of society, with two different styles, orientations, values, and forms of organizations.

One final note is required on the Latino Institute's construction of Latino ethnic identity. The story of the Latino ethnic identity and consciousness does not end with the organization's attempt to gain recognition and legitimation as a middle-class entity, serving as the voice of the wider "Latino community." We can only accept this form of Latino consciousness as another expression or fashion in the process of creating and recreating this kind of group form. Conversely, the formulation of a Latino Institute does not mean the disappearance of the "Latino grass-roots efforts" of local-level community organizers. Instead, the Latino Institute is part (and not the end) of a story about the situational merging of a multiethnic group into one collectivity and how the different actors (in this case the middle-class segment of the Latino population) construct this type of group identity.

5

Latino Ethnic Consciousness in a Broader Context

On the whole the study provides two dimensions, which I believe, are central to the understanding of the concept of Latino or Hispanic as a distinct type of ethnic identity and behavior. First and foremost, the study's data reflect the fact that the respondents' ideological formulations of Latino ethnic consciousness and identity are situationally specific in their expression. From this point of view Latino ethnic identification is operative in the sequences of social situations through which members of at least two Spanish-speaking groupings pass in the course of their urban existence and experiences. The Latino ethnic solidarity provides a particular form of intergroup relations among two or more Spanish-speaking populations; it ascribes them, according to the situation, to a relationship of incorporation, in which the boundaries of individual groups are crossed over and a larger-scale unit is formed.

And Latino or Hispanic ethnic identity is viewed and expressed by the study's respondents as a political phenomenon: a strategy to attain the needs and wants of the groups. The politicization of a situational Latino ethnic identity and consciousness suggests that the sense of this group form emerges and waxes in periods when the interests of this collectivity can be better advanced by this new "cultural" or "linguistic" innovation. The emerging interest-group conception of Latinismo or Hispanismo may appear difficult to define since individual Puerto Rican, Mexican American, and Cuban ethnics represent interest groups themselves. However, when these individual ethnic interests are the same and it is agreed that they can be better advanced or protected via certain concerted efforts among Spanish-speaking populations, the salience and affinity of the wider Latino unit is manifested.

The politicization of a situational Latino ethnic identity and consciousness also entails a dialectical process. It stresses, ideologizes, and sometimes virtually re-creates the distinctive and unique national-cultural identities of the various groups before the "taking-on" of a Latino ethnic-conscious identity and behavior. Conversely, this would mean that the "smallest-scale identities" are not impediments to organization on the basis of a wider Latino identity. The formation process of Latino ethnic identification preserves individual and separate group ethnic ties at the same time as it emphasizes a wider or global identity and consciousness by transforming the groups into a wider, politically mobilized population.

In sum, the Latino or Hispanic boundary is a highly conscious cleavage and a new mode of interest-articulation for Spanish-surnamed groups. The formation and expression of Latino ethnic identity and consciousness is a part of the mobilization process, created and initiated by leaders, and it usually crystallizes under conditions of shared structural commonalities among two or more Spanish-speaking ethnics.

Another important point needs to be added here. It is obviously clear that the particular cases of the Spanish Coalition for Jobs and the Latino Institute both appear to be examples of the type of ethnic change in which preexisting national and cultural ethnic identities have been utilized in new ways to realize objective goals. The two cases add up to a major contribution to specifying the components of identity and behavior that are subject to change, the ideological symbols that can be used by different Spanish-speaking groups to promote and protect their interests, and the conditions that influence changes in the content and salience of Latino ethnic identity. The two cases also point to the formation of Latino ethnic identity. It was shown in chapter 2 that individual Puerto Rican and Mexican American ethnic boundaries originally were clearly evident in the daily routines of the area residents. While in some circumstances Puerto Ricans and Mexican Americans were in constant physical contact and were tolerant of one another, their daily life was still demarcated by individual ethnic boundaries. Puerto Rican or Mexican American ethnicity circumscribed social interaction in the churches, clubs, taverns, and recreational areas of each neighborhood. People tended to limit their interaction to their kind, particularly in the case of their primary relationships as well as their social action. National ethnicity was a basis for personal trust for individual Mexican American or Puerto Rican residents, and the personal bonds prompted by ethnic consciousness of kind were vital to social interaction and mobilization in the individual communities, for otherwise the residents had little reason for crossing their respective ethnic boundaries. This began to change as significant similarities in the experiences of Puerto Ricans and Mexican Americans, coupled with the influence of the Affirmative Action policy, led to successive organizing and mobilizing efforts among the groups. This, in turn, led to various attempts on the part of community organization leaders, as in the case of the Spanish Coalition for Jobs and Latino Institute, to forge a Latino or Hispanic ethnic identity by claiming common interests and shared structural similarities.

And, finally, the study's empirical evidence suggests further that in the final analysis it is also the changing consciousness of the Spanish-speaking that defines Latino or Hispanic ethnic identity and behavior. For the Spanish-speaking today ethnicity is no longer this or that national or cultural commitment per se of the individual group; rather it has also become the perceived Latino inequalities and inequities in regard to access to and possession of economic, educational, political, administrative, and social resources. For the person who is Latino ethnic conscious the expression of Latino ethnic identity suggests that particular Spanish-speaking persons have built relatively enduring interpersonal ties based in large measure on the common agreement to recognize one another as belonging to the same "Latino ethnic membership category." This further suggests that in their contacts such persons have come to invest in, and come to value, resources which they can term "Latino," and that the overall net of such connected relationships will form an elementary nexus of social order within which these groups or persons can organize, in part, their way of life in American society.

LATINO ETHNICITY AND OTHER ETHNIC EXPERIENCES

In addition to the foregoing observations, the book has also described what might be considered a somewhat special case of ethnicity or ethnic-group formation. The fact that Latino ethnic identity is situationally operative and not based on one genuine national/cultural heritage passed down through the generations makes the representation of it nonetheless real for Spanish-speaking groups. The evidence presented in this study basically suggests that the cultural symbols of the Latino ethnic unit are quite fluid and not fixed in space or time. Viewed somewhat differently, rather than deriving from historically fixed cultural ties, the collective representations that adhere to the Latino ethnic identity and consciousness come from the observation of the strategic reactions of "disadvantaged" people and groups to their assignment to underprivileged statuses offered within the context of this society's political economy.

The development and expression of Latino ethnic behavior and consciousness are far from constituting a unique case of the process of developing and using ethnicity as a strategic possibility in the larger society. There are some very notable parallels between the creation of Latino ethnic consciousness and the emergence of other ethnic identities in this country.

First and foremost, practically all immigrant groups and their descendants turned to their ethnicity as a strategic solution to their conditions in urban America. Irish immigrants to Chicago represent one example. The Irish were the second-largest group of newcomers to Chicago during the nineteenth century—second only to German immigrants. Beginning as canal diggers and laborers, the Irish soon came to dominate the city's political system as they also did in the larger cities of the Northeast. Irish familiarity with British election procedures and their ability to speak the language of the host society, combined with the expansion of the urban political system at the time of their arrival, provided them with an advantage in this area. Further, Chicago Irish control of city politics was eased by the existence of numerous political factions fighting for party supremacy in this midwestern metropolis. Funchion (1981:22) explains how the rivalry within the contending political parties facilitated Irish participation in the city's political structure:

> Perhaps because of its rapid growth rate, or perhaps because of a confusing set of overlapping city, county, and township jurisdictions, late nineteenth-century Chicago had a fragmented system of politics. Neither the Republicans, who dominated the city council, nor the Democrats, who occupied the mayor's office more than the GOP did, were controlled by a centralized political machine like New York's Tammany Hall. Instead, each party was divided into a motley array of factions, or 'mini-machines,' which were continually involved in making deals with one another. In fact, on the local level at least, deals frequently occurred across party lines: the spoils of office took precedence over party loyalty.

Thus, with a decentralized political system operative in Chicago, the Irish had a golden opportunity to operate as an "ethnic minipolitical machine," wheeling and dealing with various Democratic and Republican factions. Subsequently, the Irish in Chicago, like those in other cities, gave the bulk of their support to the Democratic party, which in turn relied on their support and loyalty in their competition against the Republicans. Unquestionably the correlation between Irish ethnicity and politics in Chicago is quite apparent. "By 1890 . . . when they made up just 17 percent of the city's population, the Irish held at least twenty-three of the sixty-eight seats on the city council" (Funchion, 1981:22). This resulted in their disproportionate control of city departments such as the police and fire as well as many other city jobs. The significance of Irish hegemony in Chicago politics is explicitly stated by Green (1981:220):

> Irish politicians, with clannish determination, distributed the spoils of the city government—jobs, contracts, and insurance—long before any political organization had set up a city-wide patronage system to reward its members. No other ethnic group remained as steadfast to its own as the Irish; and whereas other newcomers marveled at this loyalty, the Irish merely looked on it as a fact of life.

Second, there are some similarities between the development of Latino ethnic consciousness and the creation of the ethnic identities of the southern and eastern European groups in this country. "Their group concepts of ethnic identity," writes Hannerz, "only emerged in the [American] urban environment, as the immigrants were not used to identifying themselves in terms of nationalities or origin which were in some cases recently established and rather artificial" (1974:43).

The Italian immigrants serve as the classic case of a group which came to the United States from relatively isolated rural areas and were most apt to identify themselves as the people of certain villages, towns, and provinces. In most instances their "peer group relations" (Gans, 1962) and other social relationships were based on village and provincial ties. This point is clearly illustrated by Nelli (1970:xiii) in his study of Italians in Chicago:

> Most of Chicago's Italians came from that area of the Kingdom lying south of Rome (especially the provinces of Aguila, Campabasso, Avellino, Potenza, Cosenza, Reggio, Catanzaro, and Bari) and the western portion of Sicily. Immense differences in history, geography, and language among and within these regions promoted loyalty to the native village rather than to the Kingdom of Italy. Homeland or paese meant village of birth, outside of which lived strangers and enemies. Residents of other towns or provinces, regarded as foreigners, became objects of suspicion or contempt. This narrow perspective broke down in American cities, where new patterns and institutions influenced habits and outlooks. Of necessity, immigrants joined together in benefit societies, churches, and political clubs; they lived and worked in surroundings crowded with non-Italian strangers; their children attended schools filled with 'outsiders.' They read the same Italian language newspapers, and they came to regard themselves as members of the Italian community.

In much the same way, it is safe to say that at this time in history the kind of Latino ethnic identity and consciousness described in this study may have relatively little to do with Latin America. It seems clear that this group identification is largely a phenomenon of American urban life: that is to say, it has in fact emerged as an American urban phenomenon because the consciousness-of-kind was aroused by the encounter of the Spanish-speaking with systems of racism and inequality in this society. The data showed how different urban contexts and the social-class levels of the leaders of the Spanish-speaking communities in Chicago influenced the construction and expression of Latino ethnic identity and social relationships among Puerto Ricans and Mexican Americans.

Third, there is also a parallel to the ethnic political consciousness associated with black minority experiences in the United States. For both the Spanish-speaking population and blacks an emergent and collective group identity has permitted the strategic use of a consciousness-of-kind that in the past was not homogeneous. In this sense Latino ethnic consciousness may correspond to Brown's (1935) articulation of black racial reality. He said: "Through race consciousness the members of a race become a historical group acquiring a past, aware of a present and aspiring to a future. A racially conscious group is more than a mere aggregation of individuals zoologically distinguishable from other ethnic groups. It is a social unit struggling for status in society. It is thus a conflict group, and race consciousness itself is a result of conflict" (quoted in Pitts, 1974:668).

Fourth, and perhaps more importantly, the interethnic process of relationship among Spanish-speaking ethnics in Chicago, which leads to the development of a distinct form of Latino ethnic mobilization, has comparative significance to other experiences of interethnic solidarity in this country. The nearest parallel is with Native Americans. The experiences of resettlement on reservations, of battles with whites, and of struggles for access to traditional lands and treaty rights endured by Indian tribes in America have been forged together in legends and myths as the basis for a "pan-Indian identity." Trosper, for instance, argues that while American Indians have roots in many different groups or tribes, many Indians today claim to share a common identity on the basis of having a common "mythlike charter" which he defines as a "historical event, or series of similar historical events, that, when used in [different] ways, aid ethnic mobilization" (1981:247). In more specific terms, Trosper points to the symbolic actions associated with the occupation of the Island of Alcatraz in the late 1960s as an important example of the efforts on the part of Indian leaders to formulate a pan-Indian identity. Drawing upon the experiences of the occupation of Alcatraz and the subsequent forcible eviction of those involved, Trosper also indicates that Indian writers and speakers have invested formulations of a pan-Indian identity with an emotional quality that echoes other emotional experiences in the history of Indian relations with non-Indians (1981:248-49).

While Spanish-surnamed groups as one population do not share an equivalent parallel to the Native American experience, they have relied on other symbolic themes in formulating the Latino or Hispanic unity. The primary symbolic content of the Latino or Hispanic identity is the Spanish language, which, in turn, is used to give public expression to what is asserted to be the common heritage of all "Latinos" or "Hispanics." (The symbolic or actual role of the Spanish language in the formulation of the Latino boundary will be discussed below.)

Like all of these ethnic experiences, the concept of Latino or Hispanic has come to represent an ethnic identification and consciousness which glorifies and crystallizes a new collectively made up of Puerto Ricans, Mexican Americans, Cubans, and others: the proclivity of multiethnic Spanish-speaking groups to seize shared socioeconomic and political similarities as a definition of a wider identity. In so doing, individual Spanish-speaking groups identify and classify not only those of their respective groups but also the goals and consequences of an interethnic social relation.

LATINO ETHNIC-GROUP FORMATION

Interest in the examination of the formation process of "Latino ethnic-group identity and consciousness" has received little attention from journalists, scholars, or the general public for a number of reasons. One reason seems to be the influence of the definition of the concept of Latino or Hispanic used by federal and local government bureaucracies and the electronic and printed press. These institutions tend to label or categorize the Spanish-speaking as a homogeneous population on the basis of a shared-language similarity. That Latinismo or Hispanismo now represents, at least for certain groups and at some times, more than a mere term applied for the sake of convenience by outsiders is demonstrated by the participation of Puerto Ricans and Mexican Americans in "Latino organizations" such as the Spanish Coalition for Jobs and the Latino Institute in the city of Chicago.

Another reason why the study of Latino or Hispanic ethnic identity and consciousness has been obscured is that, in general, most studies of intergroup relationships in this country have been more concerned with the maintenance of ethnic boundaries and expressions of competition or conflict, both symbolic and actual (Glazer and Moynihan, 1963; Gordon, 1964). Thus, theoretical models have not been developed to explore those possibilities in ethnic relations when a flow of individuals among groups takes place to create new ethnic innovations such as Latino ethnic identity. (Nagel, 1982, is perhaps the exception.)

And the final reason for the neglect of the study of the formation process of Latino ethnic identity and behavior seems to be that ethnic boundaries for the various individual Spanish-speaking groupings are often viewed as being fairly rigidly structured. In other words, given the very different backgrounds of Spanish-speaking groups, given the continuing salience of such identities as Puerto Rican, Mexican American, Cuban, and so on, and given the very different interest situations in which the groups find themselves, it is not surprising to find that the concept of Latino or Hispanic is regarded with apprehension by some people, as if its very recognition would replace the various groups' individual national and cultural heritage, as well as each group's interests and concerns. It is important to recognize that the notion of Latino ethnic identity does not represent a particular strategy to solve problems of identity, belief, and culture. In other words, the idea of Latino ethnic identification should not be perceived as a threat to the "conscience collective," as Durkheim (1964) refers to the cultural values and norms that separate one group from others, but rather it should reflect a conceptual commitment to explore those conditions which encourage the expression of a multiethnic group form. As Greeley (1974:130) emphasizes, "identification, heritage, and culture apparently inter-relate in different ways at different times in the natural history of an ethnic group."

These various observations indicate, however, that bringing people from diverse ethnic groups together within a Latino or Hispanic boundary is a challenging task. Thus, serious exploration of the process by which Latino affinity and behavior comes into being must be guided by a theory that establishes it as an ethnic unit, separate and distinct from the individual boundaries and identities of various Spanish-surnamed ethnics. In developing this theoretical/analytical framework two major challenges must be met: (1) determining the extent to which the concept of Latino or Hispanic can be viewed as a wider, multiethnic identity and (2) determining the extent to which members from the different populations, while maintaining their individual identities, interact across their boundaries.

The first mechanism recognizes that the unique potential of Latinismo or Hispanismo for mobilizing Spanish-speaking people as a collective "political force" must stem from its appeal to sentiments of "common origin." The potential of the concept of Latino as a mobilizing force lies in its ability to arouse emotions and loyalties founded on people's real or assumed ethnic ties. This view is convergent with Hechter's perspective (1978:304) which advances that "ethnic group solidarity must be indicated by the strength of sentiments binding individuals into a collectivity; it alludes to the quality of relations existing among individuals sharing certain cultural markers." The same perspective is reflected in Smith's definition of "ethnic movements":

> Ethnic movements make their claims in virtue of an alleged 'community of culture,' in which the members are both united

> with each other by a shared culture and differentiated from others by the possession of that culture. They are, moreover, different not only from their rulers, but also from their neighbours in one or more significant cultural dimension. It is in virtue of this real or alleged culture individuality that ethnic movements claim a communal solidarity and the recognition of their political demands.

Latino ethnic identity, then, needs to be based upon the reality or myth of unique culture ties which serve to demarcate them from other groups or populations. In turn, this would further mean defining Latinismo or Hispanismo within the wider concept of "ethnicity"—itself an elusive idea difficult to define with precision (Isajiw, 1974; Cohen; 1974; and others).

There are two leading approaches used by social scientists to define the concept of ethnicity: (1) one conceives of it as implying a cultural heritage shared by a group and (2) the other views it as a form of social organization that functions to achieve ends for a group of people. These two approaches have been referred to in different ways by different people, that is, primordialist vs. circumstantialist (Glazer and Moynihan, 1975); primordial vs. ideological (Shils, 1957); nonrational vs. rational and subjective vs. objective (see Burgess, 1978). For the purpose of this discussion I will refer to the cultural (primordialist, nonrational, and subjective) approach as the "traditionalist" view and the social organization (circumstantialist, ideological, rational, and objective) model as the "emergent" theory.

In specific terms, the emergent theory seeks to understand ethnicity as a developmental phenomenon: an adaptive response to external forces rather than the manifestation of a preconscious impulse. For example, Yancey et al. maintain that ethnicity is best understood as an emergent form of group identity which "may have relatively little to do with Europe, Asia and Africa, but much more to do with the exigencies of survival and the structure of opportunity in this country" (1976:400). Similarly, Fischer demonstrates how ethnic identities are intensified by urbanism, as distinguishable in-migrant populations to urban areas reach a "critical mass," enabling them to create and sustain a variety of specialized institutions and services which "structure, envelop, protect and foster their subcultures" (1975:26). In short, the emergent approach regards ethnicity as a dependent variable, created by a broad combination of external interests and strategies, which invest it with a potential for action and mobilization.

To the supporters of the traditionalist view ethnicity represents one element of an individual's basic identity: ethnicity is inherited. This traditional definition of ethnicity focuses on the transplanted cultural heritage as the principal antecedent and defining characteristic of ethnic groups. For instance, Isaacs (1975:32) suggests that ethnic identity is made part of the individual even before he attains consciousness: it is an inheritance. Bernard (1972:3), in his discussion of American immigrants and ethnicity, refers to ethnic groups in the following way:

> Ethnic groups are people who have been brought up together under a particular cultural roof. They share the same ways of doing things, the same beliefs and institutions, the same language and historical background. What they have is not derived from any special biological or genetic traits, but comes to them as part of their cultural heritage, formed out of common responses to common needs in the historical experience of their group.

Barth (1969) follows an essentially similar line, seeing ethnic categories as classifying persons in terms of their "basic most general identity" as determined by their origin and background. And Gordon argues that because "society insists on its inalienable ascription from cradle to grave, a sense of ethnicity cannot be shed, like class, by social mobility" (1975:87).

These are the major principles of the traditionalist and emergent explanations of ethnicity. Their predictions differ markedly. I suggest that a combination of the two models provides the most adequate framework for the analytical study of Latino or Hispanic ethnic identity. This means, then, that in the process of establishing the concept of Latino in ethnic terms, forms of shared-cultural and social-structural similarities be evident.

As a starting point, the Spanish language can be made to represent the "primordialized" dimension of Latino ethnic identity. That is to say, the Spanish language would serve as the characteristic symbolizing the cultural similarities of Mexican Americans, Puerto Ricans, Cubans, and others. In addition to establishing the Spanish language as the "cultural feature" that can be taken as the essential element of the cultural heritage of the Latino or Hispanic ethnic group, it is just as important to recognize that Latino ethnic identity is related more to the symbol of the Spanish language than to its actual use by all members of the various groups. Or, as in the words of Rothschild (1981:26), "What is at stake here is not simply the right or the pressure to use this or that language as a medium of communication but the whole issue of access to power and status for the respective contending ethnic groups—in the other words, the politicization of ethnicity."

This approach to the study of the role of the Spanish language in shaping the Latino identity also shares a striking similarity to the sort of attenuated ethnic sentiment and sense of identity which Gans (1979) has dubbed "symbolic ethnicity." According to Gans educated third- and fourth-generation ethnics are inventing new modes of ethnic identification, despite the growth in intermarriage across ethnic lines and the decline of any remaining ethnic occupational ties. For these ethnics the original ethnic cultures brought to America by their grandfathers and great-grandfathers are irrelevant to their everyday lives but retain an emotive aura and provide materials out of which they can construct for themselves and their present needs a new ethnic identity. Symbolic identification for third- and fourth-generation

Italians, Irish, Polish, Jewish, and others is found in such diverse phenomena as ethnic *rites de passage* and ceremonial, ethnic foods and consumer goods, and ethnic characters on TV and films. Even traumatic historical events like the Holocaust may serve the function of providing a symbolic identity for those Americans who no longer possess a real group identity or practice a genuine ethnic culture.

Indeed, there are many examples of symbolic ethnicity the world over. De Vos' observation regarding the "Gaelic" language is one such example: "The Irish use Gaelic as a symbol of their Celtic ethnicity, as do the Scots, but speaking Gaelic is not essential to group membership in either case" (1975:15). Another case is presented by Ragin (1977). From a more general context he writes (1977:440):

> Obviously, one does not construct an identity out of thin air. One builds on what one finds—in terms of language, religion, and distinctive life-styles. Nonetheless, it is quite clear that both linguistic and religious homogeneity and passion (a fortiori devotion to separate life-styles) are social creations which cannot be accounted for as simple continuities of tradition eternal. They are social creations, molded with difficulty in times of travail.

It is also significantly important to establish the Spanish language in primordial or cultural terms, since without cultural ties the concept of Latino or Hispanic will only represent expressions of a particular interest group. Conversely, without interest attachments cultural sentiments would not yield a lively, self-conscious Latino identity for the Spanish-speaking. In effect, without a cultural dimension one cannot begin to locate ethnic categories, such as Hispanic or Latino ethnicity, in society; nor would one be able to differentiate particular ethnic groups from others. This point is clearly indicated by Schildkrout (1974:192):

> Like the closely related concept descent, ethnicity minimally implies a set of social categories giving rise to communities whose members may or may not have distinct subcultures.

> However, in terms of the larger society of which the ethnic communities are a part, the boundaries of ethnic communities are culturally defined. Ethnic group boundaries consist of symbols, and it is perhaps even more important they be understood by outsiders than they be accepted by the members themselves.

While I am persuaded that the sharing of the Spanish language may provide one of the underlying motivations that lead members of this population to seek solidarity with those whom they recognize as being "of the same people" or as "sharing the same culture," such recognition, I would emphasize, is predicated upon the interplay between this aspect and the structural similarities shared by these groups. In other words, I maintain that we should not regard cultural elements such as the Spanish language, as in the case of Mexican Americans, Puerto Ricans, Cubans, and so on, as defining characteristics of the Latino ethnic unit. The language similarity shared by the various Spanish-speaking groups does not bring about a collective response to their collective needs and wants, and without these motivations the different groups may remain uncoordinated and atomized. Rothschild's (1981:27) discussion of the limitations of primordial ties as mobilizing agents for ethnic groups reflects my point:

> But initially these markers are simply the assumed givens of life, not in themselves sufficient (though necessary) to mobilize those who share them in self-conscious groups that will be internally cohesive and externally competitive. Such mobilization occurs when these given cultural markers are infused with an intense, differentiating value, are elevated into an ethnic ideology. Thereafter the language or religion or customs or pigmentation are no longer simply 'the way we do things,' or 'the way we are,' but are appreciated as uniquely precious, binding those who share them into a special community pursuing collective goals.

Further, if one chooses to regard the language similarities among Spanish-speaking groups as their primary characteristics, this would entail, following Barth's (1969:15) argument, a "prejudged viewpoint both on (1) the nature of continuity in time of such units, and (2) the locus of the factors which determine the form of the units."

Thus, that these populations speak the same language is not sufficient to influence or bring about the creation of a Latino or Hispanic ethnic identity and consciousness; instead, the construction and expression of this type of group identification and behavior is dependent upon the influence or effect of structural factors such as systems of inequality, discrimination, racism, and the like on the groups' shared-cultural and linguistic similarity. These commonalities, in turn, are excited into Latino ethnic mobilization by certain external stimuli such as Affirmative Action as in the case of the Spanish Coalition for Jobs.

In the main, these structural conditions combine to serve as the forces which spark the creation and expression of Latino or Hispanic ethnic identity and solidarity. As a result, these very same factors make of the concept of Latino a form of emergent ethnicity: Latino ethnicity is an emergent expression of shared structural and cultural feelings, excited as a strategic, wider-scale unit by disadvantaged people as a new mode of seeking political redress in American society.

Overall, when combined into one theoretical framework, the traditionalist and emergent perspectives of ethnicity suggest that a Latino ethnic group is not merely a collectivity of persons who speak Spanish; nor is it merely an association of individuals whose common interests bring them together in cooperation and symbolic unity. A Latino ethnic group is a political interest population with something extra: the belief by its members that their condition is the result of the effect of structural conditions and forces on their shared linguistic identity. Thus, the important point for those attempting to formulate a Latino ethnic identity as an inclusive ethnic identity is that symbolic means must be found to suggest to people not that they are members of a group merely because they have common interests, but rather that they unavoidably have common interests because they are all the same people. From this point of view an attack on one of the groups is seen as an example of the relationship of the entire group to outsiders—it could happen to any of us—rather than as something that distinguishes one group from the others.

The other mechanism contributing to the formation of Latino solidarity is the extent to which members interact across the boundaries of their own group. Before proceeding, it is important to define the concept of "ethnic solidarity," since some observers make an analytical distinction between it and processes such as ethnic mobilization. "Ethnic solidarity is defined," according to Olzak (1983:356), "as the conscious identification with a given ethnic population and includes the maintenance of strong ethnic interaction networks and institutions that socialize new members and reinforce social ties." From this point of view participation and density of interaction in community organizations will be used as the particular measure of Latino ethnic solidarity, that is, the most critical locus of interaction among Spanish-speaking groups is the community organization.

This study indicates that for Mexican Americans and Puerto Ricans in Chicago the community organization has come to represent the significant social process from which they are learning what it means to be "Latinos" or "Hispanics." In other words, the empirical evidence suggests that it is community organizing, or other similar kinds of group associations and actions involving the participation of more than one Spanish-speaking group, that brings forth Latino ethnic identity and solidarity among Puerto Ricans and Mexican Americans in Chicago. As indicated above, participation in community organizations can contribute to Latino ethnic solidarity by establishing settings for multigroup contact and interaction that can strengthen ties among individuals of different Spanish-speaking ethnicities. The community organization can also provide these individuals with a set of common material interests that can serve to reinforce informal, intergroup social ties.

The significance of community organizations and group associations in producing a sense of Latino identity and solidarity is also demonstrated in how Puerto Rican and Mexican American community organization leaders have learned to use a Latino group identity to optimize the political influence of a wider collectivity which is politically and economically disadvantaged. These leaders witnessed that blacks, excluded from electoral participation, for example, sought through boycotts and sit-ins to bring an end to segregation and racial discrimination. This and other examples reveal that on both national and local levels citizens of all racial/ethnic and national backgrounds have united around common characteristics and attitudes in efforts to change their conditions in urban America. A concern about the urban problems of Spanish-speaking residents in Chicago led almost inevitably to an interest in developing "Latino community organizations." As was shown in earlier chapters, governmental policies influenced Spanish-speaking community organizations in Chicago to become mobilized almost as quasi-political parties (Wilson, 1973) during the early years of the 1970s decade. These structures coalesced and proceeded to develop an alternate means of political representation (the organization of a "Latino front") in the face of a lack of elected representatives or the failure of elected representatives to respond to their needs and concerns.

In brief, it appears abundantly clear that at this time in history the supporters and promoters of the Latino or Hispanic ethnic identity are the leaders of community organizations and similar groups who attempt to organize or coordinate and coalesce the different segments of the larger Spanish-speaking population. In other words, the leadership of community organizations and institutions appears to be the leading force behind the promotion and development of internal and external bonds and cohesion among the Spanish-speaking in response to the conditions of urban life.

In the analysis of the social construction of Latino or

Hispanic ethnic identity and solidarity by community organization leaders one needs to consider the possible limitations that may be inherent in this type of group form. In other words, since the Latino ethnic identification is shaped primarily by the leadership of the various community organizations, one may expect resistence to Latinismo or Hispanismo if these leaders are unable to link Mexican American or Puerto Rican identity to Latino identity. How leaders recreate or expand ethnic identities is one of Smith's (1981) major concerns in his discussion of the role of elites in the making of an ethnic group. This sentiment is expressed in his analysis of the transformation of a religious group into an ethnic community (1981:98):

> There are . . . difficulties in this metamorphosis. The populations of the faithful may not easily fit into this kind of historicist scheme, being either too large or too small or too scattered and divided for ethnic convenience. That has been the trouble with many 'pan' nationalisms, but none more so than that of pan-Islamism, which has had to compete, not only with other linguistically based 'pan' movements like pan-Arabism or pan-Turkism, but also with the nationalism of the several states into which Arabic- and Turkic-speaking peoples have been divided, many of whom possess their own specific histories apart from the general history of the Islamic umma or the 'Arab nation.' These complications weaken the binding power, if not the fervour, of latterday pan-Islamic crusades, and make it well-nigh impossible to organize the Muslim faithful into a politically coherent movement.

One way out of this problem or challenge, according to Smith, is to use the "historicist and evolutionary framework" in the analysis of ethnic identities. The central feature of the concept of "historicism" is a predilection for interpreting individual and social phenomena as the product of sequences of events which unfold the identity and laws of those phenomena. The function of historicism in terms of giving meaning to the concept of ethnicity is concisely explained by Smith (1981:89-90):

> For the peoples of Asia, Africa and America, history furnished the vital clue to their identities, and historicism provided a framework of meaning to their distinctive characteristics. The historical and evolutionary framework has served the essential purpose of endowing with meaning and coherence what might otherwise easily be seen as unrelated pieces of cultural information and markers.

From this point of view Latinismo or Hispanismo can be conceptualized as an identity which unfolds in a time sequence. The process of Latino ethnic formation, that is, the intergroup relationship of two or more Spanish-speaking groups, cannot be confused with eventual cultural integration or merger. This process, usually termed acculturation by anthropologists, is assumed to occur when groups of individuals having different cultures come into continuous first-hand contact, with subsequent changes in the original culture patterns of either or both groups (Redfield, 1936). As noted earlier, the expression of Latino ethnic identity and behavior does not entail that the salience of individual Mexican American and Puerto Rican ethnicities will be neutralized or suppressed. However formulated and presented, what is at stake here is that the certain elements or symbols of Latino ethnic identity must be appropriated and internalized by individual Mexican Americans and Puerto Ricans before they can serve as the basis for orienting them to social action as Latinos or Hispanics. This is to say that part of the means of effecting unity among Spanish-speaking people is the formulation of a suitable symbol of identity. By manipulating the symbols of Latino group identity community leaders can inspire sentiments conducive to collective action. This observation leads directly to the following questions: What is the symbolic content of Latino ethnic identity? What are the sources of the symbols that compose them and the concepts they represent? and How is the difference in the nature of the contact situation for Spanish-speaking related to the availability of meaningful symbols of Latino ethnic identity and solidarity? This difference, I will argue, has direct significance for the possibility of the creation of Latino ethnic solidarity.

Several symbols recognized as potential sources of unifying sentiment for Spanish-speaking were discussed in earlier chapters. These unifying symbols can be grouped into two broad categories: common interests, expressed as the need to unify for collective or mutual benefit, and common identity, as the basis for doing so. (It is important to keep in mind that the latter category refers to the need to establish the concept of Latino or Hispanic as itself ethnic.) When community organization leaders succeed in establishing the two as closely interlinked, the Latino ethnic identity may be particularly effective.

FURTHERING THE EMPIRICAL STUDY OF LATINISMO

In this last section of the chapter I will indicate some fruitful lines to pursue in social-science research on Latino ethnic identity as it is expressed in certain regions of the country as well as at the national level. Before pursuing this discussion, it is instructive to note one major, relevant aspect to this concern. This study's theoretical/conceptual framework is meant to represent one possible model to be used in the analysis of the universe of Spanish-speaking experiences in the United States. In other words, this theoretical model should not be perceived as the only tool available for the study of the different types of intergroup relationships developed among different Spanish-speaking groups. After all, it is quite apparent that the situation of Mexican Americans and Puerto Ricans in Chicago represent only one case or example of intergroup relations in a society comprised of a much larger and diverse Spanish-speaking population. It was mentioned earlier, for example, that for these two groups subordination and oppression became subjects of symbolic interpretations and were made part of the foundation of Latino or Hispanic ethnic identity and solidarity in this midwestern metropolis. But while some Spanish-speaking groups are objects of the most extreme forms of discrimination and racism, even these vary according to sectional/regional differences. There may very well be particular Spanish-speaking groups who do not experience the same kind of oppressive conditions. Viewed differently, the Spanish-speaking population is divided by socioeconomic status, regions, life-styles, and, more importantly for some, by national and cultural ties, symbolic and putative. Social life in the different regions of the country, sectors of work, schooling, home, and religion may be compartmentalized, so that the process of the Latinocization of these regional, sectional, and status-diversed populations may be quite different from the one examined in this study. Despite these wide differences, for the Spanish-speaking in the United States today the concern remains: To what extent the Latino or Hispanic category can be defined and used as a valid national identity? Let us turn to the task of outlining specific directions for addressing this concern.

These new directions seem important for several reasons. As implied in the preceding paragraph, it is safe to say that at the time of this writing there may not be a national Latino ethnic movement to speak of. Although many individual Spanish-speaking ethnics are found living in segregated communities in different regions of the country and continue to experience the very same structural inequalities as they occupy subordinate roles, these individual groupings are not oriented or mobilized as a national Latino or Hispanic collectivity and afford no basis for Latino programs and movements nationally. It may be safe to say, as suggested earlier, that we have the beginnings of a Latino ethnic identity and consciousness but not, as yet, its developed form. In other words, what appears to exist are local or regional types of Latino ethnic identification processes and expressions, waiting to be transformed into a national form. There is certainly a great deal of hope for this transformation, since this stage is characteristic of early phases of any group consciousness or the incipiency of any social movement (cf. Park and Burgess, 1924:866-67). It appears, almost clearly, that it becomes part of the work of the social scientist to further the conceptual and empirical understanding of Latinismo to help facilitate this transformation.

These new directions are also important to us both from an applied view and from the viewpoint of social science itself. Central to both viewpoints is a commitment to the understanding of the dynamics of intergroup relations among Puerto Ricans, Mexican Americans, Cubans, and other Spanish-speaking groups. From the applied side, understanding leads to better modes of management and mobilization; from the social-science side, understanding leads to furtherance of our knowledge of the concept of Latinismo as well as of the generic concept of ethnicity.

In providing specific directions for furthering the study of the concept of Latino or Hispanic I shall argue for the utility of a particular approach which subsumes recent developments among the Spanish-speaking under the more generic concepts of Latinos. In other words, special attention is given to identifying conceptually appropriate units of analysis and available data for the study of behavior which I have termed throughout this study as Latino-related.

A. *Latino Ethnic Consciousness and Research*

There are several other factors to consider when using the concept of Latino ethnic consciousness in empirical research so as to distinguish it from the distinct and separate Puerto Rican, Mexican American, Cuban, and Central and South American identities. First, my findings indicate that Latino consciousness is contextual or situational; that is, the creation and sharing of a Latino identity occurs during those situations when two or more Spanish-speaking ethnics unite to advance their collective interests or to resolve a problem that affects them in the same way. Accordingly, only analytically distinct dimensions of the behavioral activities of Puerto Ricans, Mexican Americans, Cubans, and Central and South Americans involve the notion of Latino ethnic consciousness. That is to say, Latino ethnic identification is not the combination of various groups' behavioral patterns, nor does it persist independent of their intergroup social behavior. Rather, Latinismo represents a collective-generated behavior which transcends the individual group's national and cultural identities.

The situational dimension of Latino ethnic consciousness, then, represents an important consideration to keep in mind when this type of group form is used in empirical research. The researcher needs to be aware of those situations when the Latino ethnic identity manifests itself, emphasizing those instances when at least two Spanish-speaking groups coalesce or merge as one collectivity.

Second, the researcher should focus on the degree of conformity by members of this larger collectivity to certain patterns of normative behavior in the course of their intergroup relationships. By patterns of normative behavior I am referring here to the symbolic social formations and activities (i.e., the stereotypes, mythologies, slogans, theories, ideologies, etc.) found or expressed in social contexts such as community organizing, coalitions, networks, and other types of group associations. The point presented here is that available everyday artifacts should be regarded as appropriate data for the systematic study of the process of group consciousness-making.

Several of these symbolic and ideological sentiments were noted in pamphlets, memorandums, leaflets, and other kinds of literature used by a group of Puerto Rican and Mexican American community organization leaders to promote Latino ethnic consciousness in Chicago in the early 1970s. Part of the speech of Tomas Chavez, representing LA RAZA Caucus at the "Latino Strategies for the '70's" conference, discussed in chapter four, is one example:

> When I was living in Michigan I used to visit a Latino friend in the hospital who was dying of cancer. The nurses used to

enter in their daily sheets the following entry: 'Sleeps well and never complains. Sleeping and never complains.'

This Latino was sleeping and never complained. This is the diagnosis which this society always makes of us. . . . Today I want to make a proclamation. I want you to recognize a truth—that a new day has come. 'THE SIESTA IS OVER' !!! The *Brown Skin Latino* [italics are mine] has awakened and he will never be the same again (Reprinted in "Latino Strategies for the '70's—Report," June 1, 1973:4)

Third, when using the idea of Latino ethnic consciousness in empirical research, it is instructive to keep in mind that this type of group form and identity is always oriented toward advancing the collective interests of the groups. In other words, the Spanish-speaking adopt a Latino identity to gain advantages or overcome disadvantages in the larger American society: Latinismo is *political ethnicity*, a manipulative device for the pursuit of collective political, economic, and social interests in society.

As a political type of group consciousness, Latinismo or Hispanismo implies that the Spanish-speaking can improve their condition by uniting as a larger numerical "Latino group." Accordingly, the researcher must be aware of the issues around which Latino ethnic behavior is reflected. Currently the necessary conditions for the manifestation and expression of Latino ethnic consciousness arise in the areas of jobs, housing, education, and the like.

Fourth, the situational feature of Latinismo as well as its issue-oriented dimension further imply that this type of collective identity is operative in urban settings such as Chicago where two or more Spanish-speaking groups are centrally located. In such settings the Latino or Hispanic ethnic identity will tend to form on the basis of existing networks of interaction. This means, in Homans' (1950) terms, that there will be a positive relationship between the intensity of interaction among a set of individuals and the degree to which group solidarity develops.

Conversely, this means that if the populations are spatially dispersed, as is the case with Puerto Ricans in New York,

Mexican Americans in the Southwest, and Cubans in Miami, the general level of interaction within it will tend to be low, as will its degree of group solidarity. Further, distance can also act to make some groups or individuals more "peripheral" to networks of interaction than others who are more centrally located. Thus, as noted earlier, Latino or Hispanic group formation among Puerto Ricans, Mexican Americans, Cubans, and others is determined by interaction rates which, in turn, are affected by the spatial organization of the aggregate. To the extent that these conditions fail to be met prospects for Latino or Hispanic group solidarity are diminished.

This is not to suggest that the manifestation of the Latino or Hispanic ethnic identity is operative only in Chicago or that it can only be analytically understood in this urban center. The point advanced here is that if we regard Latino ethnic identity and behavior as a product of intergroup social relationships, we thereby eliminate the consideration of viewing it simply as a label. To speak in the United States of someone as Italian American is usually to call to mind for speaker and listener a set of attributes that are assumed to be Italian. Preferences for certain foods and beverages or for particular kinds of music might be conveyed, either separately or together, by the single word "Italian." Not only are such ethnic labels markers that single out individuals and categorize them, but they provide us with a kind of shorthand explanation.

Using ethnic labels to classify people and explain their behavior implies a belief that people behave similarly because they share a similar nature. That is to say, when we use ethnic labels in this way, we are subscribing to the view that Italians are essentially alike, as are Greeks, or Jews, or Germans. This also tends to reinforce the aspect of ethnicity that centers on a belief, by insiders, that members of a given ethnic category share a common origin, cultural or genetic. They act similarly because they are alike.

Ethnic labeling, however, need not be destructive; it can help to reinforce or supplement ethnic consciousness. My basic point is that when using ethnic labels, Latinismo or Hispanismo provides us with a taken-for-granted reality. It does not afford means for ordering social relationships among Spanish-speaking groups, nor does it explain the behavior in these groups' relationships.

Furthermore, as an ethnic label, Latino ethnic consciousness is simply the significance that is attributed to perceptible cultural distinctions insofar as public manifestations are concerned. As such it is beyond further analysis and must remain a primordial basis of definition in the same way that sex is: it cannot be reduced to a more elemental form. Patterson (1975:306) expressed a similar concern about the study of ethnicity:

> Most definitions of the term [ethnicity) have been descriptive and static in an attempt to isolate a set of characteristics or traits by which the term may be delineated. Herein lies much of the confusion. Such definitions emphasize culture and tradition as the critical elements, and in so doing, are so descriptive that they become analytically useless, and often so inclusive that they are not even worthwhile as heuristic devices. Cultural attributes are of no intrinsic interest from a dynamic structural perspective. . . . A theory of ethnic cultural elements and symbols is an absurdity, because these symbols are purely arbitrary and unique to each case.

It is argued here that Latino ethnic consciousness be viewed as a "contextual" category, that is, as a general principle that illuminates the behavior of persons from the various groups in specified social situations. Since in the Northeast, Southwest, and Florida only one group represents the Spanish-speaking population of the region (that is, numerically speaking), the idea of a Latino ethnic group identity will have both theoretical and practical significance only when these groups transcend their respective regional boundaries and interact at the national level as one Latino unit.

From this point of view "contextualization" becomes an important concept in studying Latino ethnic identity and behavior, for the context itself must become an integral part of the study. Yancey et al., for example, identified several key variables as being especially important in their effects on the expression of ethnicity: (1) occupational niche, (2) residential stability and concentration, (3) institutional affiliation, and (4) historical period. These "intervening variables" adhere in various combinations and intensities according to the large context such as the ecological nature of the city, process of industrialization, and modernization (1976: 392). By reference to a particular larger urban context or structure one can define the shared arena of interaction among Spanish-speaking ethnics rather than simply focusing on a single group. The key empirical question suggested here concerns the contextual relationship among two or more Spanish-speaking groups and the general prospects for political mobilization. It will be assumed that in the absence of such contexts Latino ethnic mobilization is not a certainty.

B. Program for Studying Latino Ethnic Behavior

In addition to the directions outlined above there are several other data bases which can be used in an analysis of Latino ethnic behavior. First, it is instructive to reflect on the types of data on institutionalized racial and language inequality. That is, emphasis should be given to the inequality which defines the social groups in society and "has always been mediated through and buttressed by institutions, not by persons behaving as individuals" (Pitts, 1974:675). This type of data will indicate to the researcher "how various segments of the population [can be] sociologically linked together through unequal participation in the society's economic and political institutions" (Pitts, 1974:675).

Second, data should be collected on the types of relationships among the Spanish-speaking organizations or leadership and their social positions or bases which determine that relationship. This means specifying the objectives, programs, and tactics of the organizations which mediate their relationships. In my own study I found that those organizations with compatible programs and tactics viewed the idea of a Latino ethnic identity similarly. Conversely, there is a difference among organizations with different programs and tactics in terms of how they define and use the idea of Latino ethnic behavior. Like Pitts (1974:674) it is argued here that the "failure to gather data on relationships and interactions among [these groups] sets up an interpretative situation in which undesirable sentiments seem explainable in terms of stereotypes about social disorganization among [social groups]."

Third, in addition to community organizations other groups and institutions which have specialized "Latino programs and services," such as churches, foundations, and universities, often provide the setting for the study of Latino ethnic group identity. The Spanish-speaking persons that participate in these associations have yet to be systematically researched from the vantage point of sharing and exhibiting a Latino ethnic behavior.

Fourth, a variety of recent actions, symbols, and activities have allowed for the expression of Latino ethnic consciousness. The bilingual education movement is one obvious example. The Spanish-speaking press, television, radio programs, national conventions of Spanish-speaking educators, and the like are just a few of the other recent activities which remain unexamined.

The present discussion is an attempt to encourage critical assessments of the study of the concept of a Latino collective ethnic identity. It argues for a new way of using this group form in research. Rather than a theoretical understanding of Latino ethnic behavior as the expression of one Spanish-speaking group's identity, it argues for a program of study which focuses on its collective and emergent character.

Notes

INTRODUCTION

1. A total of 34 representatives from Puerto Rican and Mexican American community organizations and social-service agencies were interviewed by the author. There were several instances when respondents were interviewed more than once; on three occasions the respondent was interviewed three times. One of the most difficult tasks of the research was that of compiling a relatively exhaustive list of Spanish-speaking organizations. The problem was partially resolved by the Latino Institute which provided me with a list of Spanish-speaking organizations it had compiled in April 1980. This list became the initial source used to approximate the universe of Spanish-speaking organizations in Chicago: 105 organizations were listed. Walton and Salces compiled a "rank order" of those organizations recognized by other organization leaders as the "most important in carrying out activities and representing the Latino communities" (1977:44). A total of 38 organizations were recognized as such; I decided to use this hierarchy of Spanish-speaking community organizations for the research. Several of these organizations were found to be out of service, reducing the initial number to only 27. Finally, to this number were added those organizations and social service agencies which were not listed or in existence when the Walton-Salces study was conducted.

2. A classic example is provided by John Burma's study (1954). Giving the impression of being a study of Latinismo, that is, of the collective identification of Spanish-speaking groups in this

country, his book is actually an accumulation of facts about several distinct groups of "Spanish Americans" and Filipinos as well. A similar approach used in the examination of a Latino or Hispanic community is evident in two or more recent studies specifically about Chicago's Spanish-speaking populations: *The Political Organization of Chicago's Latino Communities* by Walton and Salces (1977) and *Aqui Estamos* by Lucas (1978). In both cases the concept of Latino or Hispanic as a singular corporate identity for the Spanish-speaking population is never examined. Walton and Salces' only mention of it is found in a footnote at the outset of their discussion: "here we shall use the term 'Latino' to describe Chicago's Spanish-speaking population in the aggregate since, according to our data, it is most preferred" (1977:1). Lucas, on the other hand, says flatly: "Popularly, the term *Latino* has been used quite often to describe this population (the Spanish-speaking), and related cultural manifestations. It will be used in this report."

3. The selection of Mexican American and Puerto Rican community organizations for the study was done exclusively for methodological reasons. Primarily this was because there were no more than three or four Cuban community organizations and/or Central and South American organizations servicing this other component of the Spanish-speaking population in the city of Chicago. Thus, to have included these in the study would have given it a conceptually irrelevant style or sample.

CHAPTER 3

1. One major point of concern here has to do with the recognition that the term or label of "Latino" has been used prior to the 1970s by some individuals. My focus is on the social uses of the term in promoting the interests and concerns of the Spanish-speaking collectively and not on whether a person from the Spanish-speaking *barrios* or from outside the groups uses this category to label someone who happens to speak Spanish. Furthermore, obviously like all social categories, ethnic categories presuppose some amount of consensus. I am concerned, not with the quantitative dimension of this, but only with the fact that once the categories exist, behavior may be based upon recognition of

them. Latino ethnicity is relevant in a social situation even if only a set of actors acknowledge its existence and act according to the norms or stereotypes that they associate with this categorization.

Bibliography

BOOKS

Alinsky, Saul. 1969. *Reveille for Radicals* (New York: Vintage Books).

______. 1972 *Rules for Radicals* (New York: Random House).

Bailey, Barry and Ellis Katz. 1969. *Ethnic Group Politics* (Columbus: Charles F. Merrill)

Banfield, Edward and James Q. Wilson. 1963. *City Politics* (Cambridge, Mass.: Harvard University Press and MIT Press).

Barrera, Mario. 1979. *Race and Class in the Southwest: A Theory of Inequality* (Notre Dame, Ind.: University of Notre Dame Press).

Burgess, Ernest W. and Donald J. Bogue, eds. 1964. *Contributions to Urban Sociology* (Chicago: University of Chicago Press).

Burma, John H. 1954. *Spanish-Speaking Groups in the United States* (Durham: Duke University Press).

Daherendorf, Ralf. 1959. *Class and Class Conflict in Industrial Society* (Stanford, Calif.: Stanford University Press).

Dahl, Robert. 1956. *A Preface to Democratic Theory* (Chicago: University of Chicago Press).

______. 1961. *Who Governs? Democracy and Power in an American City* (New Haven: Yale University Press).

Downs, Anthony. 1973. *Opening Up the Suburbs* (New Haven: Yale University Press).

Durkheim, Emile, 1964. *The Division of Labor in Society* (New York: Free Press).

Enloe, Cynthia H. 1980. *Police, Military and Ethnicity: Foundations of State Power* (New Brunswick, N.J.: Transaction Books).

Fish, John H. 1973. *Black Power/White Control: The Struggle of the Woodlawn Organization in Chicago* (Princeton, N.J.: Princeton University Press).

Frazier, Franklin E. 1966. *The Negro Family in the United States* (Chicago: University of Chicago Press).

Frohlich, Norman et al. 1971. *Political Leadership and Collective Goods* (Princeton, N.J.: Princeton University Press).

Gans, Herbert J. 1962. *The Urban Villagers: Group and Class in the Life of Italian-Americans* (New York: Free Press).

Glazer, Nathan. 1975. *Affirmative Discrimination: Ethnic Inequality and Public Policy* (New York: Basic Books).

______ and Daniel P. Moynihan. 1963. *Beyond the Melting Pot,* rev. ed. 1970. (Cambridge, Mass.: MIT Press).

Gosnell, Harold. 1967. *Negro Politicians: The Rise of Negro Politics in Chicago* (Chicago: University of Chicago Press).

Greeley, Andrew. 1974. *Ethnicity in the United States* (New York: Wiley).

Greenstone, J. David and Paul F. Peterson. 1973. *Race and Authority in Urban Politics* (New York: Russell Sage Foundation).

Greenwood, David J. 1973. *Unrewarding Wealth: The Commercialization and Collapse of Agriculture in a Spanish Basque Town* (New York: Cambridge University Press).

Hawkins, Brett and Robert Lorinskas. 1969. *The Ethnic Factor in American Politics* (Colombus: Charles F. Merrill).

Hernandez-Alvarez, Jose. 1967. *Return Migration to Puerto Rico* (Berkeley, Calif.: Berkeley Institution of International Studies, University of California).

Homans, George C. 1950. *The Human Group* (New York: Harcourt Brace).

Lipsky, Michael. 1971. *Protest in City Politics* (Chicago: Rand McNally).

McCarthy, John and Mayer Zald. 1973. *The Trend of Social Movements in America: Professionalization and Resource Mobilization* (Morristown, N.J.: General Learning Press).

Myrdal, Gunnar. 1944. *An American Dilemma: The Negro and Modern Democracy* (New York: Harper and Row).

Nelli, Humbert S. 1970. *Italians in Chicago: 1880-1930, A Study in Ethnic Mobility* (New York: Oxford University Press).

Padilla, Felix M. *The Changing Nature of Puerto Rican Ethnic Consciousness in Chicago 1948-1980* (forthcoming).

Park, Robert E. and Ernest W. Burgess. 1924. *Introduction to the Science of Sociology* (Chicago: University of Chicago Press).

Pierce, Bessie Louise. 1957. *A History of Chicago,* vol. 3, *The Rise of a Modern City 1871-1893* (Chicago: University of Chicago Press).

Redfield, Robert. 1956. *Peasant Society and Culture: An Anthropological Approach to Civilization* (Chicago: University of Chicago Press).

Rothschild, Joseph. 1981. *Ethnopolitics: A Conceptual Framework* (New York: Columbia University Press).

Schermerhorn, Richard. 1970. *Comparative Ethnic Relations* (New York: Random House).

Schneider, Eugene W. 1969. *Industrial Sociology: The Social Relations of Industry and the Community*, 2nd ed. (New York: McGraw-Hill).

Smith, Anthony D. 1981. *The Ethnic Revival* (New York: Cambridge University Press).

Taylor, Paul S. 1932. *Mexican Labor in the United States: Chicago and Calumet Region* (Berkeley: University of California Press).

Walton, John and Luis M. Salces. 1977. *The Political Organization of Chicago's Latino Communities* (Evanston, Il.: Northwestern University Center for Urban Affairs).

Wilson, James Q. 1973. *Political Organization* (New York: Basic Books).

Wirth, Louis. 1928. *The Ghetto* (Chicago: University of Chicago Press).

ARTICLES IN PERIODICALS AND EDITED COLLECTIONS

Año Nuevo de Kerr, Louise. 1975. "Chicano Settlements in Chicago: A Brief History," *Journal of Ethnic Studies*, vol. 2, no. 4 (Winter): 22-32.

Barth, Frederick. 1969. "Introduction," in Frederick Barth, ed., *Ethnic Groups and Boundaries: The Social Organization of Cultural Difference* (London: George Allen & Unwin): 1-12.

Belenchia, Joanne. 1982. "Latinos and Chicago Politics," in Samuel K. Gove and Louis H. Masotti, eds., *After Daley: Chicago Politics in Transition* (Chicago: University of Illinois Press): 118-145.

Bell, Daniel. 1975. "Ethnicity and Social Change," in Nathan Glazer and Daniel P. Moynihan, eds., *Ethnicity: Theory and Practice* (Cambridge, Mass.: Harvard University Press): 141-174.

Bernard, William S. 1972. "Integration and Ethnicity," in William S. Bernard, ed., *Immigrants and Ethnicity: Ten Years of Changing Thought* (New York: American Immigration and Citizenship Conference): 1-7.

Boehm, Max H. 1933. "Nationalism," *Encyclopedia of the Social Sciences*, vol. 11 (New York: Macmillan): 227-240.

Bowles, Samuel. 1973. "Understanding Unequal Economic Opportunity," *American Economic Review*, (May): 346-356.

______. 1971. "Unequal Education and the Social Division of Labor," *The Review of Radical Political Economics*, 3 (Fall-Winter): 38-66.

Burgess, Elaine M. 1978. "The Resurgence of Ethnicity: Myth or Reality?" *Ethnic and Racial Studies*, 1 (July): 265-285.

Cohen, Abner. 1974. "Introduction: The Lesson of Ethnicity," in Abner Cohen, ed., *Urban Ethnicity* (New York: Tavistock Publications): ix-xxiv.

Devereaux, George. 1975. "Ethnic Identity: Its Logical Foundations," in George De Vos, ed., *Ethnic Identity: Cultural Continuities and Change* (Palo Alto, Calif.: Mayfield Publishing House): 42-70.

De Vos, George. 1975. "Ethnic Pluralism: Conflict and Accommodation," in George De Vos, ed., *Ethnic Identity: Cultural Continuities and Change*: 5-41.

Enloe, Cynthia. 1981. "The Growth of the State and Ethnic Mobilization: The American Experience," *Ethnic and Racial Studies*, vol. 4, no. 2: 123-136.

Fischer, Claude. 1975. "Toward a Subcultural Theory of Urbanism," *American Journal of Sociology*, 80 (May): 1319-1341.

Freeman, Jo. 1983. "On the Origins of Social Movements," in

Jo Freeman, ed., *Social Movements of the Sixties and Seventies* (New York: Longman): 8-30.

Funchion, Michael F. 1981. "Irish Chicago: Church, Homeland, Politics and Class—The Shaping of an Ethnic Group, 1870-1900," in Peter d'A. Jones and Melvin G. Holli, eds., *Ethnic Chicago* (Grand Rapids, Mich.: Wm. B. Eerdmans): 9-39.

Gans, Herbert J. 1979. "Symbolic Ethnicity: The Future of Ethnic Groups and Cultures," *Ethnic and Racial Studies*, vol. 2, no. 1 (January): 1-20.

Gordon, Milton. 1975. "Toward a General Theory of Racial and Ethnic Group Relations," in Nathan Glazer and Daniel P. Moynihan, eds., *Ethnicity: Theory and Practice*: 84-110.

Greeley, Andrew. 1974. "Editorial," *Ethnicity*, (April): iii-iv.

Hannan, Michael T. 1979. "The Dynamics of Ethnic Boundaries in Modern States," in John W. Meyer and Michael T. Hannan, eds., *National Development and the World System* (Chicago: University of Chicago Press): 253-275.

Hechter, Michael. 1978. "A Theory of Ethnic Antagonism: The Split Labor Market," *American Journal of Sociology*, vol. 84, no 2: 293-318.

______. 1978. "Group Formation and the Cultural Division of Labor,"*American Journal of Sociology*, vol. 84, no. 2: 294-318.

Heiberg, Marianne. 1979. "External and Internal Nationalism: The Case of the Spanish Basque," in Raymond Hall, ed., *Ethnic Autonomy—Comparative Dynamics* (New York: Pergamon Press): 180-200.

Hernandez-Alvarez, Jose. 1968. "The Movement and Settlement of Puerto Rican Migrants within the United States, 1950-1960," *International Migration Review*, vol. 2, no. 2 (Spring): 40-51.

Hill, Herbert. 1977. "Federal Labor Policy and Equal Opportunity: Mandate for Change," *Civil Rights Digest*, 9 (Winter): 27-37.

Isaacs, Harold. 1975. "Basic Group Identity: The Idols of the Tribe," in Nathan Glazer and Daniel P. Moynihan, eds., *Ethnicity: Theory and Practice*: 29-52.

Isajiw, Wsevolod. 1924. "Definitions of Ethnicity," *Ethnicity*, 1: 111-124.

Kemp, Kathleen and Robert L. Lineberry. 1982. "The Last of the Great Urban Machines and the Last of the Great Urban Mayors? Chicago Politics, 1955-77," in Samuel K. Gove and Louis H. Masotti, eds., *After Daley: Chicago Politics in Transition*: 1-26.

Kerr, Louisa A. 1975. "Chicano Settlements in Chicago: A Brief History," *Journal of Ethnic Studies*, (Winter): 22-32.

Kilson, Martin. 1972. "Black Politics: A New Power," in Irving Howe and Michael Harrington, eds., *The Seventies: Problems and Proposals* (New York: Harper and Row): 297-307.

______. 1975. "Blacks and Neo-Ethnicity in America," in Nathan Glazer and Daniel P. Moynihan, eds., *Ethnicity: Theory and Practice*: 234-253.

______. 1971. "Political Change in the Negro Ghetto, 1900-1940's," in Nathan I. Huggins, Martin Kilson, and Daniel M. Fox, eds., *Key Issues in the Afro-American Experience* (New York: Harcourt Brace Jovanovich).

Lopata, Helena Z. 1964. "The Function of Voluntary Associations in an Ethnic Community: 'Polonia'," in Ernest W. Burgess and Donald T. Bogue, eds., *Contributions to Urban Sociology*: 203-223.

Lyman, Stanford M. and William A. Douglass. 1973. "Ethnicity: Strategies of Collective and Individual Impression Management," *Social Research* 40: 344-365.

Maldonado, Lionel A. 1982. "Mexican Americans: The Emergence of a Minority," in Anthony G. Dworkin and Rosalind J. Dworkin, eds., *The Minority Report*, 2nd ed. (New York: Holt, Rinehart and Winston): 168-195.

McCrone, Donald J. and Richard J. Hardy. 1978. "Civil Rights Policies and the Achievement of Equality, 1948-1975," *American Journal of Political Science*, 22 (February): 1-17.

Nagel, Joane. 1982. "The Political Mobilization of Native Americans," *The Social Science Journal*, vol. 19, no. 3 (July): 37-45.

______ and Susan Olzak. 1982 "Ethnic Mobilization in New and Old States: An Extension of the Competition Model," *Social Problems*, vol. 30, no. 2 (December): 127-143.

Nielsen, Francois. 1982. "Toward a Theory of Ethnic Solidarity in Modern States." Paper read at the 1982 World Congress of Sociology in Mexico City, August 16-21.

Olzak, Susan. 1983. "Contemporary Ethnic Mobilization," in Ralph H. Turner and James F. Short, eds., *Annual Review of Sociology*, 9: 355-374.

Patterson, Orlando. 1975. "Context and Choice in Ethnic Allegiance: A Theoretical Framework and Caribbean Case Study," in Nathan Glazer and Daniel P. Moynihan, eds., *Ethnicity: Theory and Practice*: 305-349.

Pennock, J. Roland. 1968. "Political Representation: An Overview," in J. Roland Pennock, ed., *Representation* (New York: Atherton Press): 1-23.

Pitts, James. 1974. "The Study of Race Consciousness: Comments on New Directions," *American Journal of Sociology*, 80 (November): 665-687.

Prenti, Michael. 1967. "Ethnic Politics and the Persistence of Ethnic Identification," *American Political Science Review*, 61 (September): 15-29.

Ragin, Charles C. 1977. "Ethnic Political Mobilization: The Welsh Case," *American Sociological Review*, 44 (August): 619-635.

______. 1977. "Class, Status, and Reactive Ethnic Cleavages; The Social Bases of Political Regionalism," *American Sociological Review*, 42 (June): 438-450.

Reich, Michael. 1977. "The Economics of Racism," in David Gordon, ed., *Problems in Political Economy* (Lexington, Mass.: D.C. Heath): 183-187.

______. 1972. "The Evolution of the U.S. Labor Force," in Richard Edwards, Michael Reich, and Thomas E. Weisskopf, eds., *The Capitalist System* (Englewood Cliffs, N.J.: Prentice-Hall): 29-43.

Rubin, Lillian. 1967. "Maximum Feasible Participation: The Origins, Implications, and Present Status," *Poverty and Human Resource Abstracts*, 2 (Nov.-Dec.): 27-39.

Salisbury, Robert H. 1969. "An Exchange Theory of Interest Groups," *Midwest Journal of Political Science*, 13 (February): 1-32.

Schermerhorn, Richard. 1974. "Ethnicity in the Perspective of the Sociology of Knowledge," *Ethnicity*, 1 (April): 1-14.

Schildkrout, Enid. 1974. "Ethnicity and Generational Differences among Urban Immigrants in Ghana," in Abner Cohen, ed., *Urban Ethnicity*: 187-222.

Shils, Edward. 1957. "Primordial, Personal, Sacred, and Civil Ties," *British Journal of Sociology*, (June): 13-145.

Silberman, Charles E. 1968. "The Mixed-Up War on Poverty," in Chaim I. Waxman, *Poverty, Power and Politics* (New York: Grosset): 112-134.

Trosper, Ronald L. 1981. "American Indian Nationalism and Frontier Expansion," in Charles F. Keyes, ed., *Ethnic Change* (Seattle: University of Washington Press): 246-270.

Trow, Martin. 1966. "The Second Transformation of American Secondary Education," in Reinhard Bendix and Seymour Martin Lipset, eds., *Class, Status, and Power,* 2nd ed. (New York: Free Press): 437-448.

Turner, Ralph H. 1970. "Determinants of Social Movement Strategies," in Tamotsu Shibutani, ed., *Human Nature and Collective Behavior* (Englewood Cliffs, N.J.: Prentice-Hall): 145-164.

Warren, Roland L. 1956. "Towards a Reformulation of Community Theory," *Human Organization*, vol. 15, no. 2 (Summer): 8-11.

Wilson, James Q. 1968. "Introduction," in Harold Gosnell, ed., *Machine Politics: Chicago Model*, rev. ed. (Chicago: University of Chicago Press): v-xiii.

______. 1961. "The Strategy of Protest: Problems of Negro Civic Action," *Journal of Conflict Revolution*, (September): 291-303.

______. 1972. "Race Relations Models and Explanations of Ghetto Behavior," in Peter Rose, ed., *Nation of Nations: The Ethnic Experience and Racial Crisis* (New York: Random House): 259-275.

Yancey, William et al. 1976. "Emergent Ethnicity: A Review and Reformulation," *American Sociological Review*, 41 (June): 391-403.

ARTICLES IN NEWSPAPERS AND MAGAZINES

"Bell Telephone Co. Increases Its Number of Latin Employees," *Booster Newspaper* (June 17, 1972).

"Boicott a la Jewel por Tiempo Indefinido," *El Informador Newspaper*, Chicago, IL. (May 13, 1974).

"Chicago Tribune Magazine." 1981. *Chicago Tribune*, Section 9 (Nov. 1).

Chicago Reporter. 1975. "Reporter Survey Identifies 18 Chicago Latino Leaders Considered Most Influential in Their Community," vol. 4, no. 7 (July): 6-9.

"Cops Brutal in Arrest: Latin Group." 1965. *Chicago Daily News* (August).

"Jewel y la Politica Arbitraria," *Chicago-San Juan*, Chicago, IL. (May, 1973).

"Latinos Beset Bell Aides with Job Demands," *Chicago Sun-Times* (September 15, 1971).

"N.O.W.—Newsletter of the Archdiocesan Latin American Committee." (Chicago, IL.: Archdiocese of Chicago).

"PROPA: Award Banquet." 1973. (Chicago, Il.: September 19).

"Victoria Para Los Hispanos." 1971. "Latin-American Coalition Against Panic-Peddling." (Flyer, July 20).

Watson, J. and C. N. Wheeler. 1971. "The Latins," *Chicago Sun-Times* (September 12-20).

GOVERNMENT PUBLICATIONS

U.S. Commission on Civil Rights. 1973. "Federal Civil Rights Enforcement Effort" (Washington, D.C.).

______. 1976. "Puerto Ricans in the Continental United States: An Uncertain Future" (Washington, D.C.).

U.S. Bureau of the Census. 1972. *Census of Population and Housing: 1970 Census Tracts*. Final Report PHC (1)-43, Chicago, IL. SMSA, Part 1 (Washington, D.C.: U.S. Government Printing Office).

______. 1973. *Census of Population*: 1970. *Subject Reports* PC (2)-1D, Persons of Spanish Surname (Washington, D.C.: U.S. Government Printing Office).

______. 1962. *U.S. Census of Population and Housing: 1960 Census Tracts*. Final Report PHC (1)-26 (Washington, D.C.: U.S. Government Printing Office).

UNPUBLISHED MATERIALS

"Acute Depression in the Latin American Community," Memo, Spanish Coalition for Jobs (Spring 1971).

"Agreement between the Building Construction Employers Associ-

ation of Chicago, Inc., and the Coalition for United Community Action," mimeographed (January 9, 1970).
Año Nuevo de Kerr, Louise. 1976. "The Chicano Experience in Chicago, 1920-1970," unpublished Ph.D. dissertation (University of Illinois, Chicago Circle Campus).
"Chicago Commons Association Annual Report: 1980-81" (November 1981).
Fish, John H. 1971. "From Conflict to Survival: A Narrative Study of the Woodlawn Organization," unpublished Ph. D. dissertation (University of Chicago).
Gordon, D. 1971. "Class, Productivity, and the Ghetto: A Study of Labor Market Stratification," unpublished Ph.D. dissertation (Harvard University).
"History of the Spanish Coalition for Jobs."
"Joint Venture Agreement: Spanish Coalition for Jobs and Jewel," mimeographed.
"Latino Institute: History and Philosophy," mimeographed (not dated).
"Latino Strategies for the '70's—Report" (February 16, 1973).
"Latino Strategies for the '70's—Report" (June 4, 1973).
Lucas, Isidro. 1978. *Aqui Estamos: An Overview of Latino Communities in Greater Chicago*. Report to Chicago United (Chicago: Chicago United).
Mollenkopf, John H. "On the Causes and Consequence of Neighborhood Mobilization." Paper presented at the Annual Meeting of the American Political Association (1973).
"Monthly Report from July 15 to August 31, 1971," Spanish Coalition for Jobs.
"Monthly Report from September 1 to October 1, 1971," Spanish Coalition for Jobs.
Nagel, Joane. 1982. "The Political Construction of Ethnicity." Revised version of paper read at the 1979 American Sociological Association meetings in Boston, August 28, 1979.
"News Release," Spanish Coalition for Jobs (July 24, 1972).
"News Release," Spanish Coalition for Jobs (August 9, 1972).
Padilla, Elena. 1947. "Puerto Rican Immigrants in New York and Chicago: A Study in Comparative Assimilation," unpublished Ph.D. dissertation (University of Chicago).
Plau, Thomas. "On the End of Community Action: How Much Does It Matter?" Policy Paper No. 12 (Center for Social

Organization Studies, University of Chicago, June 1968).
"Program of Latino Strategies for the '70's: Si se Lucha en el Presente Recordando el Pasado, el Futuro sera Nuestro" (March 16-18, 1973).
"Proposal to the Rockefeller Foundation," submitted by the Spanish Coalition for Jobs (Fall 1972).
"Progress Report, Spanish Coalition for Jobs to Chicago Commons: October, 1972, to April, 1973."
"Statement of Credibility," Latino Institute pamphlet (not dated).
"Training Contract between Jewel Tea Co. and the Spanish Coalition for Jobs."

Index

HIEBERT LIBRARY
3 6877 00114 6249